The Effective Voluntary Board of Directors

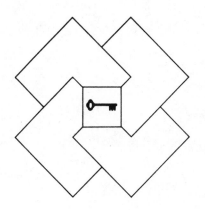

The Effective Voluntary Board of Directors

What It Is and How It Works

William R. Conrad, Jr.
and William E. Glenn

Swallow Press
Athens, Ohio   London

We wish to acknowledge Jane Lowell and Mildred Simpson of the IVO staff, who coordinated and edited the manuscript; Jill Sally, who typed the many drafts and corrections; Melinda d'Ouville who created and produced many of the graphics; and Sandra Stepler, of Authors and Speakers Service, who edited and typed the final copy.

Swallow Press Books
are published by
Ohio University Press
Athens, Ohio 45701

Library of Congress Cataloging in Publication Data

Conrad, William R.
    The effective voluntary board of directors.

    Bibliography: p.
    1. Association, institutions, etc.—Management.
2. Directors of corporations.   3. Voluntarism.
I. Glenn, William E.   II. Title.
HV41.C644   1983   658.4'22   82-8240
ISBN 0-8040-0836-1 (pbk.)

For James C. Manning

whose untimely passing took from us a beloved colleague and friend. The example of his life and the warmth of his fellowship will always inspire and guide us.

CONTENTS

Exhibits   viii
Introduction   xiii

Chapters
1   The Way of Democracy: Voluntarism   1
2   Differences Between Nonprofit and For-profit
    Organizations   6
3   The Legal Aspects of Board Membership   14
4   A Basic Management Concept for Voluntary
    Organizations and a Definition of Policy   23
5   The Organization of the Board of Directors and Board/
    Staff Relationships   47
6   The Role and Function of Committees   62
7   The Board Policy Process   77
8   The Function of the Board of Directors and the Role of
    the Board Volunteer   92
9   The Function of Staff and the Roles of Staff Members   103
10 The Delicate Balance   108
11 The Board Meeting   121
12 The Board Membership Process   128
13 Communication   161
14 Different Types of Boards and Culturally Diverse
    Voluntary Organizations   169
15 What Do I Do Now, or How To Use This Book   182
16 Conclusion   195

Appendices
I   The Bylaws   201
II   The Committee Commission   221
III The Manual of Operation   234
IV   Exhibit Availability   242
V   Bibliography   243

EXHIBITS

Chapter 2
1   First, Second, Third Sector Relationships   6
2   First, Second, Third Sector Relationships Completed   7

Chapter 3
3   Estes Rule   15
4   Bylaw Conflict of Interest Statement   16
5   Bylaw Indemnification Statement   18–19
6   Bylaw Insurance Statement   20
7   Sibley Hospital Case   20–21

Chapter 4
8   Meaning of the IVO Symbol   25
9   Management Divisions   26
10 Hierarchy of Planning   31
11 Definition of Planning   32–33
12 Planning Pyramid   34
13 Where Objectives Come From   35
14 Current Operating Issues Objectives   35
15 Justification for Objectives   36
16 The Planning Framework   37
17 Planning Framework—Management   38
18 Planning Framework—Program Services Management
    Division   39
19 Planning Framework—Resource Development (Image)
    Management Division   40

20	Planning Framework—Resource Development (Volunteer) Management Division	41
21	Planning Framework—Resource Development (Support) Management Division	42
22	Planning Framework—Business Management Division	43
23	Planning Framework—Personnel Management Division	44

Chapter 5

24	Management Divisions/Board Standing Committee Relationship	48
25	Formal Board Organization	50
26	Coordinating Committee and Executive Committee Descriptions	52
27	Board/Staff Relationships in the Basic Management Square	53
28	Basic Management Square 2	54
29	Accountability and Problem Solving	55
30	Basic Management Square: Multi-Unit Organizations (A)	58
31	Basic Management Square: Multi-Unit Organizations (B)	59

Chapter 6

32	Agenda Building and Meeting Review	66
33	Business Committee Agenda	67
34	Format for Reviewing Agenda Item	68–69
35	Sample Program Services Committee Agenda	70
36	Format for Reviewing Agenda Item	71
37	Condensed Minutes	72
38	Committee Composition	75

Chapter 7

39	Board Policy Process	79
40	The Board and Policy Implementation	80
41	Definition of Authority, Responsibility, and Accountability	81

42	Policy Formulation	83
43	Samples of Grievances	84
44	Organizational Democracy and Discipline	85
45	Executive Influence and Balance of Power	86
46	Definition of Policy for a Multi-Unit Organization	87
47	Unit Policy Flexibility in Multi-Unit Organization	88
48	Power and Control	89
49	Manipulation	90

Chapter 8
50	Governing Board Function	93
51	Role of the Board Volunteer	94
52	Three Pillars of Resource Development	95
53	Guidelines for Successful Board Volunteer Stewardship	100

Chapter 9
54	Staff Function	103
55	Role of the Staff Member in a Voluntary Organization	104
56	Enabler Role	105
57	Staff Guidelines for Successful Board Relationships	107

Chapter 10
58	The Delicate Balance—1	108
59	The Delicate Balance—2	109
60	The Delicate Balance—3	110
61	What Board Volunteers Bring to the Board/Staff Relationship	116
62	What Board Volunteers Can Reasonably Expect of Staff	117
63	Thirteen Effective Ways to Turn Off Staff	118
64	What Staff Bring to the Board/Staff Relationship	119
65	What Staff Can Reasonably Expect of Board Volunteers	119
66	Twelve Effective Ways to Turn Off Board Volunteers	120

Chapter 11

67	Board of Directors Policy Cycle	123
68	Board-Committee Meeting Cycle	124
69	Issue Flow and Assignment	125
70	Sample Board Calendar	126–27

Chapter 12

71	The Board Membership Process	130
72	Nominating Committee	133
73	Board Service Needs and Demands	137
74	Need Satisfaction	137
75	Goal Integration	138
76	Image	140
77	Optimum Composition Chart	142–43
78	Form for Candidate for Board Membership	145
79	Board Member Information Form	150–51
80	Staff Executive's Checklist	152
81	Orientation Schedule	153
82	One-Day Conference on Boards	155
83	Weekend Seminar on Boards	156

Chapter 13

84	Communication—1	161
85	Communication—2	162
86	Chain of Command	164
87	Open System	164
88	Open Chain of Command	165
89	Communications Network—1	166
90	Communications Network—2	167

Chapter 14

91	Membership Organization	170
92	Advisory Group Commission	172

93   A Culturally Common Voluntary Organization   173
94   A Culturally Diverse Voluntary Organization—1   174
95   A Culturally Diverse Voluntary Organization—2   175
96   Symbiosis of Culturally Diverse Voluntary Organizations   176

Chapter 15
97   Continuous Renewal Cycle   184
98   Force Field Model   185
99   Facilitating Forces—1   187
100   Facilitating Forces—2   188
101   Consequences Worksheet   189
102   Objectives Worksheet   191
103   Targets Worksheet   192

Chapter 16
104   Involvement–Contribution Ratio   197

INTRODUCTION

This is a book about boards. It describes what they are and how they work. It is not a book with quick answers and shortcuts.

Effective boards do not just happen. They are the result of hard work by board members and staff. However, there must be ground rules so that the hard work will be productive. That is the purpose of this book — to provide basic ground rules for effective boards.

Ten thousand copies of the first edition of this book have been distributed since its publication in 1976. In addition, the authors have conducted seminars on "The Effective Voluntary Board of Directors" in more than sixty-one cities. Some four hundred organizations and 3300 staff and board members have attended those seminars.

The authors have also consulted in scores of organizations and taught over fourteen graduate classes in "The Effective Management of Voluntary Organizations" at George William College, Downers Grove, Illinois.

The organizations represented by these contacts range across the voluntary spectrum: human services, health, hospitals, arts and education. They represent every possible structure, budget, and complexity.

This new edition has been changed on the basis of experience gained through these contacts. Every chapter includes both new and revised processes, procedures, and manuals. However, we have remained true to the basic concept from which they flow.

The many charts and procedures have passed the test of exposure and implementation. All are the result of selective evolution.

This is not to say the evolution is at an end. What follows can be improved. We hope you will do so as the opportunity arises.

We would like to share several observations made since 1976.

1. Too much time is spent saying "our board is really unique." We must realize that conceptually *all boards do the same*

things from the same set of processes. We in voluntarism must begin to recognize our similarities.

The plurality of voluntarism is in the approaches to service. The functions of the board of directors and the roles its members play are universal. What differs is the cast (staff and board) and the outcome of their deliberations (services).

We have noticed vast differences in the concepts, procedures, and operations of various boards. Profound differences exist between the member organizations of national organizations and between units of an organization within the same city.

The issue, we believe, is to establish:

Conceptual consistency; operational diversity

In other words, what is "conceptual" applies equally to the one-executive organization in a small town and to the executive of a large multi-unit operation in an urban area. The "diversity" lies in the application of the concepts. The application of concept will vary only in degree. The point is: Use the concept in whatever form is required.

2. There are too few people filling too many board slots. It is common to find people serving on five or six, even up to ten boards. "Professional" board members, those who do nothing but serve on boards, often find it hard to maintain the pace.

    For a fully employed person with other interests, service on two or three boards is about the limit.

    Beyond that number a board volunteer becomes spread too thin to know much about the organizations or to be of much practical assistance. Many cases of nonprofit mismanagement indicate symptoms of board neglect.

    Commitment cannot be cut into a slice here and a slice there.

    Additionally, the rush to the "known" or "clout" names overburdens the top and leads to the virtual untapping of the large reservoir of corporate and community people less well known. This reservoir often contains many people who *will* arrive one day. They are more important than the "arrived" because they represent the future.

3. Not enough staff time is devoted to boards. In many cases, the only individual working with a board is the staff chief executive. Unless board work is delegated to other staff where appropriate, the work of the board rarely gets done. Many staff chief executives feel reluctant to "open the board to other staff contacts." Yet, if this is not done where appropriate and with proper contacts, a board cannot function.

4. Sometimes, it seems that board and staff have MBA degrees —"Management By Ambiguity." Operational frameworks and processes are generally absent. If they do exist, they tend to be vague and contradictory. Very few voluntary organizations have integrated their boards, staff, and organizations into an operational whole.

    Frameworks, processes, flow charts, and organizational tables can be upended by strong individuals, unexpected hostilities, or coalitions.

    Further, human nature is unpredictable. No amount of planning, regardless of detail and accounting for contingencies, can ever reflect the full range of possibilities or unforeseen events.

    However, the absence of plans, processes, flow charts, and tables *insures* that strong individuals take over. The result? Often, the organization cannot respond to any unexpected events or changes.

5. Rule by oligarchy has controlled many boards. The few complain that the many never do any work, when, in fact, the few like it that way. If the many *did* become involved, the few would lose control.

    It surprises us how many board members said, "We are never asked to do anything," or "Being asked to fill envelopes once a month isn't exactly what I had in mind in board service." Remember, people will generally work if there is worthwhile work to do—and if they are asked.

These are only a few observations we have made over the course of the last few years. They are situations that should be avoided.

Working with boards is both an art *and* a science. We offer an explanation of each:

> *art:* . . . exceptional skill in conducting any human activity.[1]

> *science:* science is a way of thinking much more than it is a body of knowledge. Its goal is to find out how the world works, to seek what regularities there may be, to penetrate to the connections of things— from sub-nuclear particles, which may be the constituents of all matter, to living organisms, the human social community, and thence to the cosmos as a whole. Our intuition is by no means an infallible guide. Our perceptions may be distorted by training and prejudice or merely because of the limitations of our sense organs, which, of course, perceive directly but a small fraction of the phenomena of the world. Even so straightforward a question as whether in, the absence of friction, a pound of lead falls faster than a gram of fluff was answered incorrectly by Aristotle and almost everyone else before the time of Galileo. Science is based on experiment, on a willingness to challenge old dogma, on an openness to see the universe as it really is. Accordingly, science sometimes requires courage—at the very least the courage to question the conventional wisdom.[2]

For the staff member, working with boards is also an art and a science. Art, in that the most difficult job in the world is working with people. The art of good board work *is* "conducting human activity"— the molding of a diverse group of people into an effective whole for the good of an organization. Science, in that, to be artful, one must also be knowledgeable about *what* has to be done and what will make the parts a whole. This requires a set of concepts, procedures, roles, and functions known, understood, and agreed upon.

The successful staff member is neither wholly an artist nor wholly a scientist; he/she is a delicate blend of *both*.

This book was written to suggest some of the art and science of effective board work. The authors have tried to combine concepts (science) with "how-to" (art), and to be general enough that these concepts can be adapted to any situation.

The true pragmatist is conceptual first. Something is practical only to the extent that it operates from a proven conceptual foundation.

A few guidelines:

1. You will find references to the "Newport Organization." This is a fictitious organization we have created for the sake of

illustration. It is a youth serving organization with an administrative office, a camp, and four unit facilities.

2. We use the term *board volunteer* instead of board member, director, layman or trustee. Our reasoning is that we wish to always remind ourselves that our board members are volunteers. Sometimes we forget that.

3. We use the words *voluntary organization* to describe the nonprofit organization. Other words used are:

    nonprofit
    not-for-profit
    npo = nonprofit organization
    independent sector
    voluntarism, volunteerism
    Third Sector (the other two sectors are First Sector—business—and Second Sector—public, government.)

After one of our George Williams College classes, a student, Keith B. Andersen (now, Director of Alumni Relations), suggested that the name of the book ought to be "How to Work With a Voluntary Board Without Losing Your Program, Your Board or Your Job!" This title may seem excessively negative. Yet, it beautifully describes the delicate balance which the staff member must maintain in working with his/her board of directors:

Your Program: Preventing the program from becoming so identified with certain people or groups that it loses its validity in meeting the issues of its clients.

Your Board: Keeping the program and the various elements in harmony so that vital people or groups are both utilized and recognized thus avoiding putting the whole organization in jeopardy.

Your Job: Balancing the board and the program. A staff member should not compromise his/her own ethical base, yet should maintain this balance.

We thank Andersen for his contribution.

The following is a sample letter from a board member to the chairman of the board of directors of a voluntary organization. Although it is fictitious, it is probably safe to say that letters of this type are being written every day. If this book can prevent the writing of just one letter of this kind, the expenditure of time and effort will be well worthwhile.

Dear David:

With this letter I hereby resign from the Board of Directors of the Neighborhood Youth Organization. It is with regret that I have made this decision, and I would like to explain the reasons for this action.

Although I was surprised by the vagueness of what was expected of me when Sue asked me to serve on the Board, I was flattered and set aside my misgivings about time requirements to accept the invitation. I looked forward to our first Board meeting with enthusiasm and expectancy.

I was somewhat disappointed at that first meeting. The Board was composed of forty-nine members. There were eighteen present. Later I discovered that this attendance was considered good.

The meeting was a series of staff reports on program, budget, fund raising, and a few other matters. The only thing the Board voted on was the approval of the minutes; little discussion or Board-member participation occurred. The amazing aspect to me was how little the Board knew of the Neighborhood Youth Organization. I was new, but in discussion of NYO with other Board members—even those of long tenure —I found we all shared mutual ignorance of operations. When I asked at a Board meeting about Board committees, I found to my astonishment that I had been assigned to the Property Committee four months earlier. No one had asked me about serving on this committee, informed me of meetings, nor shared the minutes with me. I found the assignment a rather strange one for an investment banker. I also found that the committee had not met for the past fifteen months.

At the January meeting, the staff made a rather lengthy program report and presented a budget request. Then they announced a campaign goal (unrealistic, in my opinion) and exhorted the Board to raise more funds because we had missed our last year's goal. It seemed strange, in light of a failing annual campaign, that in my eight months on the Board no one had ever asked me to contribute or to raise funds on behalf of NYO. There is no need to pursue this further, except to say that I see no change from the present state of affairs in the foreseeable future. As I said earlier, I joined the Board with enthusiasm and expectancy. The opportunity to do something for our community, beyond business services, had me truly motivated. I felt I could make at least two vital contributions: means and experience.

Since becoming a Board member, I have seen many areas in which I could be helpful and useful. What has frustrated me is my inability to find the way to do so. No one has explained my responsibilities, asked my opinion, nor sought my advice. In fact, the only visit I had from anyone was when the Executive Director came to me and asked if I would host the November Board meeting in the Board dining room of my company.

I have seen the staff directing everything. It seems they not only implement policy, but, ipso facto, *make* policy. This, I believe, is contrary to the proper management of voluntary organizations.

Perhaps, the most frightening aspect of this entire situation to me, personally, is the legal aspect. Board membership carries with it the legal responsibility for an organization about which I know next to nothing, an organization which knows little about board membership, and which obviously intends to perpetuate the status quo.

As I do feel some responsibility for NYO, I am enclosing a copy of John W. Gardner's book, *Self-Renewal: The Individual and the Innovative Society*. I suggest a thorough reading of the book—and rather soon.

Sincerely yours,

Finally, we in the voluntary field simply cannot serve people on faith alone; we need systems, structures, dollars, and, above all, *people*. Without these, faith flounders and is replaced by despair and disillusionment. Any outward thrust in terms of service must be matched by effective, self-renewing systems and structures.

NOTES

1. *The Random House Dictionary of the English Language*, unabridged ed. (New York: Random House, 1967), p. 84.
2. Carl Sagan, *Broca's Brain* (Ballantine Books: New York, 1979), pp. 15-16.

THE WAY OF DEMOCRACY: VOLUNTARISM

1

. . . I do believe private institutions, where citizen volunteers work for the common or general good, form a fundamental part of the fabric of American life.

Would our life be as rich, as varied, as interesting, if services to the community were provided only by government? I doubt it. Gone would be the unique special opportunities the private agencies offer the concerned citizen for participation, through membership on boards of trustees and other support . . . to an agency.

Comment by Arthur M. Wood,
Chairman of the Board, Sears, Roebuck and Co.
Chicago, February 12, 1973

"Give me a beer an' one for Ole."
"Two malteds and one for Ole."
"Make mine cheese on rye and one for Ole."

It was noon at Rose's Cafe in a small Midwestern town. As we waited for our lunch, we heard these strange orders being given at tables all around us. "Who," we asked our waitress, "is this Ole for whom everybody seems to be ordering something?"

"Ole," she said, "is Viola Dalem. She's in St. Paul being fitted for artificial feet. She stumbled and crawled nearly three miles through the blizzard last year to get help for the thirty school children in her stalled bus. Her feet were so badly frozen that they had to amputate them last spring. Each time a customer requests "One for Ole," we put the amount of his order in that can beside the cash register and add it to his check—to help pay for Ole's new feet."

2 The Way of Democracy: Voluntarism

"And one for Ole," we said with warm emotion, as we paid our check.

—B.O.B. (Phoenix, Arizona)[1]

Of all the unique contributions made by our American civilization, the concept of voluntarism is the most worthy. It is the essence of our democracy, and, in the final analysis, the factor which will determine whether our democracy will survive—concept intact—or become just another civilization for some archaeologist to uncover in the future.

Voluntarism takes many forms. It ranges from simple acts of human concern, as illustrated in the story above, through delivery of services directly to constituents, to service on boards of directors. The French historian, Alexis de Tocqueville, perceived this over a hundred years ago when he said:

> These Americans are the most peculiar people in the world. You'll not believe it when I tell you how they behave. In a local community in their country a citizen may conceive of some need which is not being met. What does he do? He goes across the street and discusses it with his neighbor. Then what happens? A committee comes into being and then the committee begins to function on behalf of the need. You won't believe this, but it's true; all of this is done without reference to any bureaucrat. All of this is done by private citizens on their own initiative!
>
> Americans of all ages, conditions, and all dispositions consistently form associations to give entertainment, to found seminaries, to build inns, to construct churches, to diffuse books, to send out missionaries.
>
> The health of a democratic society may be measured by the quality of function performed by private citizens.

Tocqueville further referred to Americans as having an incredible sense of personal responsibility for the welfare of others—especially their youth—and the readiness to sacrifice and cooperate voluntarily and freely to support these services designed to aid others in their struggle for personal and moral maturity.

This sense of responsibility for helping others help themselves took the form of $43.31 billion philanthropic dollars in 1979, $38.77 billion of it from individuals. It also took the form of millions of volunteers contributing billions of man-hours through hundreds of thousands of voluntary organizations. If a dollar value were placed on these contributed hours, it would no doubt exceed the gross national product of the United States.

The product of this tremendous effort is millions of lives

positively affected through direct services and significant advances in the fields of social welfare, science, politics, business, labor, and every other institution in the human experience.

Professor Marshall E. Dimock once said: "Voluntarism is a good barometer of free enterprise and our American way of life. When it shows signs of decline, we are in trouble."[2]

According to John W. Gardner, the only society which will escape the archaeologist's shovel is one which is capable of self- renewal: ". . . a society that has learned the secret of renewal will be a more interesting and more vibrant society, not in some distant future but at once. And since continuous renewal depends on conditions that encourage fulfillment of the individual, it will be a society of free men." If voluntarism is the bulwark of our democracy, then the concept of self-renewal is the foundation upon which the bulwark is built.

Gardner states further: "Though the only society that can renew itself over a long period of time is a free society, this offers no grounds for complacency. We are not living up to our ideals as a free society, and we are very far from meeting the requirements of an ever-renewing society. But both are within reach."[3]

We must not allow our voluntary organizations to wither be- cause they have lost their sense of purpose, their zest for expanding the frontiers of humanity, and their willingness to explore the unknown. For, however active government may be in its combination of manpower or dollars, it is still the voluntary organization which must have the resolve, the flexibility, and the dynamism to insure that our American way of life will continue to grow and that its benefits will be shared by all its citizens. The very Founding Fathers of our country were, after all, a group of volunteers!

We, who serve voluntarism in this country, either as board volunteers or as staff members, must never forget that we are in the front lines of the struggle for democracy. In this voluntary organiza- tion we serve, we must clearly identify our purpose, goals, and objec- tives. We must establish our roles as board volunteers or staff mem- bers. We must construct systems that will not only achieve our purpose, goals, and objectives, but assure continuous renewal, as well. This is what the volunteer board is all about.

A very important book, which should be in the library of every person who cares about voluntarism, is one written by Eva Schindler- Rainman and Ronald Lippitt: *The Volunteer Community: Creative Use of Human Resources* (Fairfax, Va.: NTL/Learning Resources Corp., 1975). Appearing just before the introduction to this book is a state- ment by Edward C. Lindeman that concludes as follows:

The health of a democratic society may be measured in terms of the quality of services rendered by citizens who act in "obedience to the unenforceable."

The above phrase "obedience to the unenforceable" was in a memorable address delivered by Lord Moulton before the Authors' Club of London and later published in the *Atlantic Monthly*. "We live," said Lord Moulton, "under the discipline of three domains: one, the positive law which prescribes rules of conduct and exacts penalties for disobedience; two, the realm of free choice which is covered by no statutes; and three, that domain in which neither positive law nor free choice prevails. In this sphere the individual imposes obligations upon himself. In this realm the individual is not wholly free, since he has accepted a responsibility. Although he knows that no law and no individual may compel him to fulfill this commitment, he also knows that he cannot disobey without betraying himself. This is the domain in which the volunteer lives. The real greatness of a nation, its true civilization, is measured by the extent of this land of obedience to the unenforceable."

No discourse on democracy and voluntarism would be complete without reference to Alan Pifer's thought-provoking report: "The Jeopardy of Private Institutions" (*Annual Report for 1970/The Report of the President*, New York: Carnegie Corp., pp. 13-15). In referring to the seriousness of the position of the voluntary organization in today's society, Mr. Pifer sounds the alarm with great clarity:

In view of the state of public opinion on the question, the general lack of official concern, and the nation's preoccupation with other issues, it seems unlikely that any systematic, coherent effort will develop in the immediate future to alleviate the financial situation of private service institutions. Their relative position in our national life seems destined to decline and with it the special values they bring to our society.

Further:

Any real solution to the plight of private institutions must begin with a clear appreciation by the nation's top political leaders of what the collective presence and vitality of these institutions mean to the nation. These leaders, rather than simply mirroring public ignorance and apathy, must educate the public and, where necessary, convert it to a sense of active concern over the future of our traditional system of shared public and private effort and responsibility; and, in this task, our political leaders must be supported and reinforced by other leadership elements in the nation. Nothing less than this kind of impetus from the top will provide the basis for the great variety of measures which will be needed to preserve and revitalize the position of our private institutions.

And finally:

The time for action, whether of a broad or specific nature, is extremely late. Our historic partnership of public and private commonwealth endeavor is in grave danger because of the state of apathy that is permitting the decline of private institutions. Unless this decline is arrested and reversed, we, and our children after us, will almost certainly be living in a society where the idea of *private* initiative for the *common* good has become little but a quaint anachronism largely associated with the mores of an earlier age. Perhaps at that time, there will be Americans who are reasonably satisfied with the kinds of lives offered them by a society which functions solely through public institutions. But there may well be others with a great yearning for more variety, more choice, more animation, and more freedom, in their lives than such a system would be likely to provide. If so, they will certainly wonder at the heedlessness—the sheer negligence—of the generation before them that could have allowed a system which has these attributes to atrophy.

We who believe in and are serving the cause of voluntarism have a special responsibility to American democracy. We must ponder Mr. Pifer's somber remarks, then move to assure that our future is not the one he describes if we hold to our present course. Who is better equipped to act than we?

The social, economic, and political powers of the United States are reflected on the rosters of the boards of trustees, the boards of directors, and the committees of voluntary organizations. Collectively, this aggregate represents tremendous power and wields enormous influence. The time, as Mr. Pifer states, is late; but it not *too* late. Concerned action is required to halt the potential threat to our voluntary organizations. The means for strengthening voluntarism rests in the very system that created it: voluntary action.

NOTES

1. Reprinted with permission from "90 Best Stories From Life In These United States," Copyright 1966 by The Reader's Digest Assn., Inc.
2. David M. Church, *How to Succeed With Volunteers* (National Public Relations Council of Health and Welfare Services, Inc., 815 Second Avenue, New York, New York, 10017), p. 8.
3. John W. Gardner, *Self-Renewal: The Individual and the Innovative Society* (New York: Harper Colophon Books, 1965), p. 2.

DIFFERENCES BETWEEN NONPROFIT AND FOR-PROFIT ORGANIZATIONS

2

In the introduction, the three Sectors were introduced:

First Sector—business
Second Sector—public, government
Third Sector—voluntary, nonprofit

Before discussing the differences between the First and Third Sectors, a brief look at their relationships is necessary. The First Sector is the basic economic unit in our system. It *funds* the Second and Third Sectors. The First Sector funds the Second Sector through taxes. It funds the Third Sector through contributions, money, material, expertise and people. The Second Sector also funds the Third Sector—through grants and contracts. Diagrammatically:

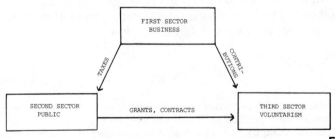

Exhibit 1

In fairness, the diagram is not complete unless it shows that a portion of the First Sector's market is the Second and Third Sectors. The Third Sector funds the Second Sector only through individual income taxes as it is exempt in all other areas. Additionally, the Second

Sector subsidizes the Third Sector through tax exemptions to the First Sector, individuals, and foundations (see exhibit 2).

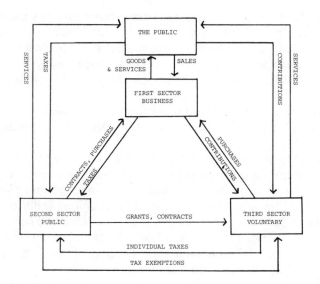

Exhibit 2

This is not designed to be a definitive economic, political, or social statement on the relationships. It is meant only to show the mutuality of interests.

Now, to discuss a few of the differences between the First and Third Sectors.

Recently, a board volunteer and an executive vice president of a major corporation said to us: "You know, I just can't get a handle on what is going on in this organization. What I find myself doing is simply raising money and looking at financial statements. We approve a budget and I'm not certain what the budget is producing. I wish they would be more businesslike."

From the staff side, many professionals complain that their board volunteers from business and industry allow conditions to exist within organizations they serve that they would never tolerate in their own businesses.

Such conditions would be alleviated if an understanding existed of the differences between the nonprofit and for-profit corporations and if boards and staff would create a system of communications which would take into consideration those differences.

Voluntary organizations tend to "look up" to business as *the* example of management while business tends to "look down" on the voluntary organization as either unmanageable or chronically mismanaged.

Both are wrong. For every successful business story there is one of failure. One only has to look at Chrysler, Lockheed, Penn Central, and the Edsel car. Joel E. Ross and Michael J. Kami wrote a significant book about business failures, *Corporate Management in Crisis: Why the Mighty Fall*. The lessons in this book also apply to voluntary organizations.

The fact is that there are a number of well managed voluntary organizations from which business might learn some management lessons.

Given the chronic lack of funds and the reliance on the good will and commitment of a broad spectrum of individuals such as board volunteers, program volunteers, politicians, and communities, the wonder is that they are managed at all. It takes unique skills to manage a voluntary organization as there are situations which do not confront the average manager in business. The type of skills required can be determined, in part, by an examination of some of the differences between for-profit and nonprofit corporations.

We are not going to place the Second Sector, or public organizations, in this comparison. However, much of what applies to voluntary organizations applies to public organizations.

1. *Marketing, Budgets and the Resource Base*

For-profit corporations are consumer oriented. This means that when a corporation markets an item, the consumer purchases it at a price that includes cost of production and a profit.

If a product does not sell, it is withdrawn and another takes its place. When nothing sells or the sales no longer cover cost, let alone profit, the result is bankruptcy.

There is a direct relationship between product and consumption.

In the voluntary organization this direct relationship does not always exist. Usually, the consumer of services does not pay for the full cost of the services rendered. This means that the money to deliver the service is provided by a third party, the public.

This is the fundamental difference between the for-profit and the nonprofit corporation, and the implications of this arrangement affect all the other differences.

This difference can be stated in another way. In the for-profit corporation, the goal is consumer satisfaction because this means profit.

The goal for voluntary organizations unfortunately is for survival. Survival does not always depend upon client satisfaction, but on the ability to attract funds. Unfortunately, the ability to attract funds is often unrelated to the service to clients.

This means a double marketing issue for voluntary organizations not faced by for-profit corporations.

The double marketing issue for voluntary organizations remains clients *and* funds. They market for funds because the clients cannot pay the full cost of the service. In marketing priorities, money will take precedence. This leads to some curious situations:

A. Fund-raising or grantsmanship seminars, publications and consultations are always more popular than those in management or programs. Success in resource acquisition has had little relationship to organizational effectiveness and efficiency.

B. Voluntary organizations are budget based. A budget has two parts, expense and income. Expenses should be based on the achievement of specific goals and objectives. Most, however, are based on items such as salaries, occupancy, and postage; or on systems such as camps, pools, gymnasiums, and trips. Expenses are rarely examined. Income is always scrutinized—again supporting the tenuous relationship between the two.

2. *Governance*

The second major difference is how the two types of corporations are governed.

Both a for-profit corporation and a voluntary organization are governed by a board of directors that is legally responsible for its respective corporation.

However, there are some significant differences:

A. The staff chief executive and staff of a voluntary organization are rarely board members. We advocate a complete separation. We believe the power of persuasion is more powerful than the power of a vote. If a staff cannot persuade a board to move in a certain direction, perhaps it shouldn't. A vote is immaterial.

B. As we will demonstrate in Chapter 4, the decisions of a voluntary board of directors go much deeper than for-profit corporations. There are the different definitions of the word *policy*.

C. There is a much greater use of committees in the voluntary organization.

D. Individual board volunteers are expected to implement certain decisions they make. As an example, unlike for-profit corporations, the voluntary board of directors funds the policy decisions it makes.

There are many business executives who find the decision-making machinery of a nonprofit organization so slow and cumbersome, with its emphasis on human relations and process, that they flatly state that the whole procedure would not work in a profit environment.

R. R. Baxter, president and chief executive officer of CF Industries in Long Grove, Illinois, does not agree with this viewpoint. Baxter manages the world's largest manufacturer and distributor of fertilizer products. CF Industries' sales topped $1 billion in 1980 with profit of $200,000,000. It has $1,003,000,000 in assets in the United States and Canada and employs 3,000. This places CF Industries 279th on the Fortune 500 in 1979.

What causes Baxter's conviction that nonprofit management can succeed in the for-profit sector? CF is a cooperative owned by 18 companies. Baxter and his key executives *are not* members of the board of directors. The chairperson of the board is elected by the board and is an officer in a member company. In this respect CF Industries, a for-profit corporation, is very similar to its nonprofit counterpart. Baxter states:

> As my top officers and I are not on the board of directors, we are as concerned about *how* a recommendation from management is brought to the board as we are with the *purpose* and *content* of the recommendation itself.
>
> If we were on the board, or a majority of the board, our approach would be highly directive. As we do not serve on our board, our approach is highly persuasive. In a persuasive mode, human relations, process and politics take on a much higher value than they do under a directive mode.
>
> This tends to slow down the decisionmaking process within management and the board; but in the long run, better decisions do result. Additionally, once a decision is made, the ownership of responsibility

for that decision is firmly fixed with the board as the process leading to a decision and management having no vote reduces the tendency to "knee jerk" approval of management recommendations.

This will not happen if the only contact we have with our directors is at board meetings.

In sum, I do not submit that the cooperative movement is not without management problems. But I do suggest that our sister for-profit and nonprofit corporations look at the cooperative where the best of both corporations have come together.

3. *Measuring Results and Accountability*

Measuring the results of work is considerably different between the profit and voluntary organization. For a profit corporation, making a profit is the basis upon which it evaluates its success and is enabled to do other things such as "social responsibility." For the voluntary organization the measurement is not so exact.

Any accounting system will tell you what a service costs. However, the measurement of its client effect and the relationship to members served is not so simple. Objectives are much more difficult to develop, write, and measure. This has led to measuring results by activity rather than by outcome. For example, we have seen objectives written: "By September 1, we will have counselled 500 children." In reality, however, this is an activity. It states only that 500 children will have received counselling. It says nothing about *what type* of counselling will be provided, *why* this counselling is important, and the *results* that are expected from it.

Similarly, many voluntary organizations have camping programs. Elaborate objectives are set for the camp. However, camps are neither objectives nor activities; they are systems. They are systems that deliver organizational objectives. Camping should be selected because it can deliver *organizational* objectives better than or in tandem with other systems such as swimming pools and gymnasiums. Chapter 4 will deal with this issue in greater detail.

Cost-effectiveness is much more difficult to measure. Voluntary organizations are much more highly labor intensive because they are dealing in human outcomes, not products. They are more highly subject to political, social, and economic trends.

All these factors make measuring results and placing accountability much more difficult for the voluntary organization.

4. *Staffing*

The educational programs for the voluntary manager and the

service provider heavily emphasize services and processes, rather than management and outcomes. Management programs that do exist include for-profit curricula which force the students to make the necessary adaptations. The results are:

A. Voluntary service providers are promoted to management positions, primarily to obtain pay raises. These people bring service-oriented approaches to management. This is not all bad. However, these managers tend to value process and procedure while business tends to look at "what it takes to get it done."

B. Because of training, voluntary managers lean toward the human relations approach to management. Again, this is not all bad. However, more emphasis is placed on human relations than the framework within which these relations are to take place and their outcomes.

C. Time and decision-making. Since client satisfaction is usually not tied to income, time becomes less important to the voluntary staff. Equal attention is given whether two or twenty-two clients are served. In business, the ability to produce so many cans of soup per hour is directly related to establishing the price of the soup to realize a profit.

In voluntary organizations, the determination is to take as much time as required to do the job because the commodity is people, not soup. This has an impact on decision-making. Without the direct income relationships, decision-making tends to become highly procedural, with as much involvement as possible. Given the need to keep the board of directors active and clients involved, this is necessary.

For-profit corporations tend to be quicker in decision-making and maintain a more clearly defined data base.

Another problem for voluntary organizations is that the staff can be highly professional. Measuring the professional worker is difficult. Issues of allegiance to the profession and allegiance to the organization can conflict.

Jobs tend to be ambiguous in the voluntary organization. Workers perform a variety of tasks. Specialization, while desired, is expensive. Hence, many workers in voluntary organizations are "multi-skilled."

The above list is not definitive. However, awareness and appreciation of these differences by a board of directors and its staff will greatly enhance the ability to work together.

THE LEGAL ASPECTS OF BOARD MEMBERSHIP

3

Important Note: The authors are not attorneys. This chapter is written to illustrate the liability issue to voluntary organizations, not to serve as the basis for decisions concerning liability. As the state laws vary greatly in approach to nonprofit liability, each organization should seek legal counsel assistance in the determination of policy for this issue. An excellent resource is:

> *Governing Board and Administrator Liability*, by Robert M. Hendrickson and Ronald Scott Mangum (American Association for Higher Education, One DuPont Circle, Suite 780, Washington, D. C. 20036).

Although the emphasis is higher education, it is applicable to all voluntary organizations. Board volunteers perform their roles in two environments: *ethical* and *moral* and *legal*. Much has been written about the ethical and moral environment. Only recently has the legal environment come to the fore.

We live in a "suit society." One only has to read the newspaper to find that someone is suing someone else for some reason. Voluntary organizations are not immune. Board volunteers are suddenly realizing that not only can the voluntary organization they serve be sued; but there are instances in which *volunteers themselves* can be sued—as individuals.

The voluntary or nonprofit organization is a corporation. In legal terms: "A for-profit or nonprofit corporation is usually considered an entity separate and distinct from its members. It is, as such, a fictitious legal person afforded the same rights and subject to the same obligations as natural persons."

The corporation, therefore, can sue or be sued in its own name. The corporate form exists, in part, to limit the individual board volunteer's liability.

The key word is *limit*. It does not say *negate*. A corporation itself, as a fictitious person, cannot carry out whatever it is empowered to do by the state. The people who carry out the power of the corporation are its board of directors and those delegated to authority by the board. The board volunteers, officers, and employees, who are authorized to act for the corporation, are its "agents."

As stated, although the corporate form protects individuals from personal liabilities, every state has penalties for "negligence."

The best protection is prevention. Prevention involves each board volunteer conscientiously performing his/her responsibilities, keeping informed of operations, and having legal counsel for advice.

The Estes Rule from *The Liabilities of Directors and Officers: With Practical Solutions for Their Discharge* by Thomas F. Sheehan (Directors Press, 260 Little John Court, Bartlett, Illinois) is shown in exhibit 3.

On Director's Liability:

Estes Rule*

$$I^3 - Se = Pm$$

Inquiry times Information times Involvement without self-enrichment leads to Peace of Mind

---

Exhibit 3

The three I's offer an excellent basis for a board volunteer's behavior in performing this role:

Inquiry: Board volunteers must *inquire* if the information they are receiving is complete and accurate. Too many board volunteers accept reports or information without comment. This habit is passive.

Information: The key—without it no responsible decision can be made.

Involvement: The information received is validated through active participation in the board volunteer role.

The term *minus self-enrichment* refers to conflict of interest. Voluntary organizations must be very careful about conflict of interest. A suit has a better chance of being won where conflict of interest exists. Voluntary organizations may avoid conflict of interest by enforcing one of two policies:

1.   No member of the board or staff, or organization as a whole, may have *any* business transaction with the organization as a group.

2.   Transactions may take place but under specific conditions as stated in the bylaws.

Exhibit 4 is a bylaw statement where transactions are permitted.

CONFLICT OF INTEREST: Any possible conflict of interest on the part of a director shall be disclosed to the board. When any such interest becomes a matter of board action, such director shall not vote or use personal influence on the matter, and shall not be counted in the quorum for a meeting at which board action is to be taken on the interest. The director may, however, briefly state a position on the matter, and answer pertinent questions of board members. The minutes of all actions taken on such matters shall clearly reflect that these requirements have been met.

Exhibit 4

In addition, it is recommended that a bidding procedure be used so that the accepted bid of a board volunteer is clearly the best choice.

Prevention means doing everything possible to reduce the likelihood of a suit being won and discouraging a suit from ever being brought. However, nothing can prevent a suit from being filed.

The following are some types of protections. These are only brief outlines:

Sovereign Immunity—This doctrine holds that a state or its agencies are immune from suit without its consent.

Charitable Immunity—It held that an organization "devoted to the public good" should be protected. This has disappeared from most states as is, and, for all practical purposes, is nonexistent.

Indemnification—This means simply that the organization assumes the obligation to pay or reimburse someone for loss or expense. Individual state law must be reviewed for this. Exhibit 5 is a sample bylaw indemnification statement.

Insurance—Insurance is simply a purchased form of indemnification. It is a policy covering each individual. Insurance can be, of course, purchased by an individual. Exhibit 6 is a bylaw statement for insurance which is part of an Indemnification Article.

Legal Counsel—While reliance on advice of counsel may not relieve a board volunteer of liability, the use of counsel can reduce the possibility of suit and liability. The attorney representing the organization should not be a board member but should be familiar with the organization.

Two important court cases for review by boards of directors are the *Wood versus Strictland* and *The Sibley Hospital* cases. These are fiduciary (financial) cases, but contain useful lessons for understanding all aspects of liability. Exhibit 7 is the first sheet of the Sibley Hospital Case. The court found the trustees individually liable for breach of fiduciary duty. Although there was no financial penalty imposed, it did set a standard for evaluation. Note particularly items 1, 2, 3, and 4.

A Short Legal Checklist:

— Are notices of meetings mailed as required by the bylaws to prevent claim that they were intentionally excluded?

— Have the minutes of board meetings been certified by the secretary and approved by the secretary and approved by the Board? They are legal documents. (See Voluntary Management Press publication: *Parliamentary Procedures*.) Are motions clearly stated and votes recorded? (Votes against any issue don't lessen liability.)

— Are all local, state and federal reports being prepared accurately and on time?

— Are budget reports and balance sheets distributed at regular intervals?

ARTICLE VII

Indemnification

7.1   ACTION BY OTHER THAN CORPORATION. The corporation shall indemnify any person who was or is a party or is threatened to be made a party to any threatened, pending, or completed action, suit or proceeding, whether civil, criminal, administrative or investigative (other than an action by or in the right of the corporation) by reason of the fact that such person is or was a director, or officer of the corporation, or is or was serving at the request of the corporation as a director or officer, of another corporation, partnership, joint venture, trust or other enterprise, against expenses (including attorneys' fees), judgments, fines and amounts paid in settlement actually and reasonably incurred by such person in connection with such action, suit or proceeding if such person acted in good faith and in a manner which such person reasonably believed to be in or not opposed to the best interests of the corporation, and with respect to any criminal action or proceeding, had no reasonable cause to believe the conduct was unlawful. The termination of any action, suit or proceeding by judgment, order, settlement, conviction, or upon a plea of *nolo contendere* or its equivalent, shall not, of itself, create a presumption that the person did not act in good faith and in a manner which the person reasonably believed to be in or not opposed to the best interests of the corporation, and, with respect to any criminal action or proceeding, had reasonable cause to believe that the person's conduct was unlawful.

7.2   ACTION BY CORPORATION. The corporation shall indemnify any person who was or is a party or is threatened to be made a party to any threatened, pending or completed action or suit by or in the right of the corporation to procure a judgment in its favor by reason of the fact that such person is or was a director or officer, of the corporation, or is or was serving at the request of the corporation as a director or officer of another corporation, partnership, joint venture, trust or other enterprise against expenses (including attorneys' fees) actually and reasonably incurred in connection with the defense or settlement of such action or suit if such person acted in good faith and in a manner such person reasonably believed to be in or not opposed to the best interests of the corporation and except that no indemnification shall be made in respect of any claim, issue or matter as to which such person shall have been adjudged to be liable for willful negligence or misconduct in the performance of duty to the corporation unless and only to the extent

Exhibit 5a

that the court in which such action or suit was brought shall determine upon application that despite the adjudication of liability but in view of all the circumstances of the case, such person is fairly and reasonably entitled to indemnity for such expenses which the court shall deem proper.

7.3   EXPENSES. To the extent that a director or officer has been successful on the merits or otherwise in defense of any action, suit or proceeding referred to in Sections 1 and 2 above, or in defense of any claim, issue or matter therein, such director or officer shall be indemnified against expenses (including attorneys' fees) actually and reasonably incurred in connection therewith.

7.4   PREREQUISITES. Any indemnification under Sections 1 and 2 above (unless ordered by a court) shall be made by the corporation only as authorized in the specific case upon a determination that indemnification of the director or officer is proper in the circumstances because the director or officer has met the applicable standard of conduct set forth in Sections 1 and 2. Such determination shall be made (1) by the board by a majority vote of a quorum consisting of directors who were not parties to such action, suit or proceeding, or (2) if such a quorum is not obtainable, or, even if obtainable a quorum of disinterested directors so directs, by independent legal counsel in a written action.

7.5   ADVANCES BY CORPORATION. Expenses incurred in defending a civil or criminal action, suit or proceeding may be paid by the corporation in advance of the final disposition of such action, suit or proceeding as authorized by the board in the specific case upon receipt of an undertaking by or on behalf of the director or officer, to repay such amount unless it shall ultimately be determined that the director or officer is entitled to be indemnified by the corporation as authorized in this article.

7.6   OTHER REMEDIES. The indemnification provided by this article shall not be deemed exclusive of any other rights to which such director or officer may be entitled under any agreement, vote of disinterested directors or otherwise, both as to action in an official capacity and as to action in another capacity while holding such office, and shall continue as to a person who has ceased to be a director or officer, and shall inure to the benefit of the heirs, executors and administrators of such a person.

Exhibit 5b

7.7   INSURANCE. The corporation may purchase and maintain insurance on behalf of any person who may be indemnified here against any liability asserted against such person and incurred in any capacity, or arising out of any status, for which the person may be indemnified.

Exhibit 6

IN THE UNITED STATES DISTRICT COURT FOR THE DISTRICT OF COLUMBIA

DAVID M. STERN ET AL., Plaintiffs,

v.

LUCY WEBB HAYES NATIONAL TRAINING SCHOOL FOR DEACONESSES AND MISSIONARIES, ET AL., Defendants.

Civil Action No. 267-73

ORDER

This action came on for trial before the Court and the Court having considered the briefs, arguments and evidence presented by all parties and having set forth its findings of fact and conclusions of law in a Memorandum Opinion filed herewith, it is hereby

DECLARED that each director or trustee of a charitable hospital organized under the Nonprofit Corporation Act of the District of Columbia, D.C. Code SS 29-1001 *et seq.*, has a continuing fiduciary duty of loyalty and care in the management of the hospital's fiscal and investment affairs and acts in violation of that duty if:

(1) he fails, while assigned to a particular committee of the Board having stated financial or investment responsibilities under the by-laws of the corporation, to use diligence in supervising and periodically inquiring into the actions of those officers, employees and outside experts to whom any duty to make day-to-day financial or investment decisions within such committee's responsibility has been assigned or delegated; or

Exhibit 7(a)

(2) he knowingly permits the hospital to enter into a business transaction with himself or with any corporation, partnership or association in which he holds a position as trustee, director, partner, general manager, principal officer or substantial shareholder without previously having informed all persons charged with approving that transaction of his interest or position and of any significant facts known to him indicating that the transaction might not be in the best interests of the hospital; or

(3) he actively participates in, except as required by the preceding paragraph, or votes in favor of a decision by the Board or any committee or sub-committee thereof to transact business with himself or with any corporation, partnership, or association in which he holds a position as trustee, director, partner, general manager, principal officer, or substantial shareholder; or

(4) he fails to perform his duties honestly, in good faith, and with reasonable diligence and care; and it is hereby

ORDERED that the appropriate officers and/or trustee committees of Sibley Memorial Hospital shall, prior to the next regularly scheduled meeting of the full Board of Trustees, draft and submit to the full Board, and the Board shall modify as it deem appropriate and adopt at said meeting, a written policy statement governing the utilization and investment of the Hospital's liquid assets, including cash on hand, savings and checking accounts, certificates of deposit, Treasury bonds, and investment securities; and it is further

ORDERED that the Board and its appropriate committees shall, promptly after adoption of said policy statement and periodically thereafter, review all of the Hospital's liquid assets to insure that they conform to the guidelines set forth in said policy statement; and it is further. . . .

Exhibit 7(b)

— Are all contracts current?

— Is the organization hiring qualified staff to deliver services?

— Are fund raising costs reasonable?

— Are any land or money trusts legally supervised?

— Is legal counsel *not* on the Board?

— Is the auditing firm *not* on the Board?

— Are Board actions in compliance with the bylaws?

— Are the bylaws reviewed annually?

This chapter is written to inform not to frighten. A board volunteer properly discharging his/her responsibilities has little to fear about liability.

A BASIC MANAGEMENT CONCEPT FOR
VOLUNTARY ORGANIZATIONS
AND A DEFINITION OF POLICY
4

There has been a tidal wave of writings describing what boards do, what a good board is, and what committees do. Another tidal wave discusses management, accountability, and planning.

Noticeably lacking is a focal point for all this—a point that integrates board, staff, and planning. Boards, staff, and planning are generally discussed in exhaustive detail, but rarely linked. Our Basic Management Concept attempts to provide a focal point for *all* that relates to a board and its staff.

We are often asked what process, procedure, or function we consider the *most* important to an effective board. We respond by identifying three processes which will determine whether or not a board will succeed. Numbers 2 and 3 flow from number 1. Our three are:

1. The planning process. Unless the planning process is well defined, nothing else can be achieved. It gives organizational direction, the criteria for board volunteers and staff, the basis for evaluation, and, the basis for defining policy. Without planning we are without purpose. An astounding number of board members still cannot define how the organization plans or defines its planning terms.

2. A clear understanding of the function of the board of directors and staff and the role of board volunteers and staff. Only with understanding—and acceptance—can a board function effectively with other members of the organization.

3. The board membership process. How board volunteers are elected, recruited, oriented, trained, rotated, recognized,

23

and separated is critical to a functioning board. Chapter 7 will deal with this process in detail.

The planning process is part of the basic concept. This concept has four components:

1. The IVO Symbol

2. Management Divisions

3. The Hierarchy of Planning

4. The Planning Framework

1. *The IVO Symbol*

The authors sought a logo for the Institute for Voluntary Organizations, their management consulting organization, which would illustrate their approach to the management of voluntary organizations. The result is four interlocking squares held together by a key. All IVO services and publications are based on this symbol (exhibit 8).

2. *Management Divisions*

The first question of management is "What has to be managed?" Exhibit 9 illustrates the management divisions for a voluntary organization. There may be changes of name, but *all* voluntary organizations manage the same things.

The size or type of the voluntary organization does not matter. Each must manage *all* the divisions. These two factors do, however, determine how the organization will be managed.

Larger organizations may have one staff person responsible for each part of the division. Smaller ones may have only one staff person or volunteer in charge of the division.

Universities may call program services "curriculum" and resource development "external affairs." Hospitals may call program services "patient care." *All* voluntary organizations share the same management divisions. How they manage their divisions and what they deliver as services makes each unique.

A synonym for management divisions is "function." In some management quarters, functional arrangements are dangerous because they lead to specialization and, inevitably, splinter the organization into competing components.

This consequence should be avoided, but not used as a reason to discard functions.

THE MEANING OF THE IVO SYMBOL

The IVO symbol has four interlocking squares held together by a fifth square containing a key. This symbol represents IVO's basic concept of a voluntary organization and is the basis for all IVO services and publications.

Program Services

This is the delivery of the purpose or mission of the voluntary organization to its selected clients. All direct and indirect client services are located here.

Resource Development

There are three basic resources which must be brought to a voluntary organization: *image* (what the public thinks about the voluntary organization; a blend of publicity and public relations); *volunteers*, both program (service) and board; and *support* from the public and private sector. The private sector includes annual giving, planned giving and capital giving.

Business

Sound fiscal management through the budget process, control and analysis; the management of property and equipment; and the management of investments and earning income.

Personnel

A strong personnel program designed to support all paid employees; professional, paraprofessional, service, clerical and part-time.

The above are the basic components of *any* voluntary organization. They are interlocked because they are interdependent and must function together if a voluntary organization is to succeed.

The Board Volunteer-Staff Relationship

The center key holds the key to success in voluntary organizations; the board/staff relationship. This relationship holds the voluntary organization together. When the function and roles of board volunteers and staff are clearly defined, understood and accepted, then this relationship can cause the voluntary organization to grow effectively and efficiently.

Exhibit 8

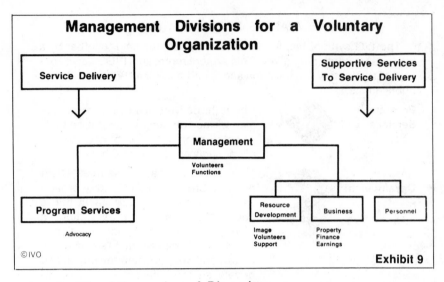

Management Divisions for a Voluntary Organization

Service Delivery

Supportive Services To Service Delivery

Management

Volunteers Functions

Program Services

Advocacy

Resource Development

Image Volunteers Support

Business

Property Finance Earnings

Personnel

©IVO

Exhibit 9

3. *The Hierarchy of Planning*

> I keep six honest serving-men
> (They taught me all I knew);
> Their names are What and Why and When
> And How and Where and Who.
>
> Rudyard Kipling

> The road of history is littered with the bones of great societies that . . . couldn't tell their druthers from their needs.
>
> Jenkin Lloyd Jones

If the management divisions are *what* has to be managed, then planning is that which provides the *process* to manage. The Hierarchy of Planning is designed to bring a common definition to planning.

Before describing the Hierarchy of Planning, a bit about planning. The rapidity of change has forced all individuals and institutions to shake themselves free from the security of the past in order to face the challenges of the future. A familiar trait in many of today's voluntary organizations is their inordinate resistance to change, i.e., planning. Although the reasons for such resistance vary, Dr. James M. Hardy, in his book *Corporate Planning for Nonprofit Organizations* (New York: Association Press, 1972, p. 1), identified four essential causes:

> First, the view that business techniques cannot be used in nonprofit organizations. Since the majority of planning theory and practice came

out of business experience, its applicability is immediately suspect in many of the organizations that have no profit motive. As Peter Drucker has pointed out, however, the practice of management is proper to the success of any organized pursuit and not at all the exclusive province of business; in fact, it is purely an accident of history that management first appeared in commerce. There are, of course, some differences in the organizational environment, but it is easy to overemphasize these and miss the opportunity to adapt learnings from one area to the other.

Second, the fact that day-to-day crises need attention, leaving little time available for planning. This is one of the most common reasons for deferring thinking about the future. Undoubtedly there are usually enough crises to occupy most or all of each executive's day and planning does require a heavy investment of executive time and energy. As one executive said, "The tyranny of the moment prevents me from paying attention to the important future of my organization." While recognizing the reality of this problem, it is vital to remember that effective planning gives an executive a structural framework of goals, objectives, and strategies, as a basis for current decision-making. Planning is valueless unless it results in current decisions that are made in light of future directions.

Third, attempting to adopt and install another organization's system or methods has not fulfilled expectations. The recognized need for corporate planning on the part of many executives has led to a search for other successful systems and a resultant preoccupation with the forms, procedures, and techniques of a "best system." This mechanical adoption of methods and procedures has invariably led to frustration, with perhaps aborting of the planning effort, and has accomplished little toward achievement of real planning for the future of the organization. The evidence clearly indicates that the emphasis must be on conceptualization and *adaptation* and not on such mechanistic adoption.

Fourth, thinking about the future is difficult and uncertain. It is especially difficult for action-minded individuals, who derive great satisfaction from doing things, to engage in long-range planning which is uncertain and fundamentally an intellectual process. Planning necessitates a mental predisposition to do things in an orderly way, to think about acting, and to act in the light of the best information available. Although assistance is available to those engaged in planning, such assistance is no substitute for the hard thinking that planning demands on the part of an organization's key leaders.

However powerful the factors of resistance are, it is the importance of planning in organizations—profit or nonprofit—which has slowly worked its way into the thinking of executives. At one time, planning was considered merely a useful tool for growth. Since voluntary organizations were usually regarded as "good," their existence was assured. Times have changed, however. Planning has escalated in importance from being a matter of *growth* to being a matter of survival.

John Gardner states: "As the organization or society ages, vitality diminishes, flexibility gives way to rigidity, creativity fades and there is a loss of capacity to meet challenges from unexpected directions."[1] Until just a few years ago, all that this meant to voluntary organizations was stagnation. Today, such a policy leads directly to the graveyard. Planning is synonymous with survival.

This chapter is not meant to be definitive in planning. The purpose is to place working with boards in a planning context by discussing planning fundamentals. Planning has as many definitions as there are those who define it. The High Lama in James Hilton's *Lost Horizon* provides a succinct definition of planning when he describes Shangri La:

> . . . we are never slaves to tradition. We have no rigidities, no inexorable rules. We do as we think fit, guided a little by the example of the past, but still more by our present wisdom, and by our clairvoyance of the future.[2]

However planning is defined, the Lama's definition provides the common characteristics of a planning definition:

1. Planning is a creative process, freed from the constraints of the past and present, yet using the past and present as resources.

2. Planning is futuristic. In it, we share a vision of what we want to be, based on our perceptions of the future and how we are going to get there. As Peter Drucker says: "Action is always aimed at results in the future."[3]

The above is perhaps an oversimplification; but unless these two characteristics are somehow contained in a planning definition, true planning cannot take place.

Planning has arisen as a way to measure accountability. Many donors are now asking for "Five Year Plans." This has caused crisis and panic—thus, a headlong rush to "planning." Three problems emerge from "crisis planning."

1. Planning is not placed in the perspective of the fundamental issues with which a voluntary organization must concern itself; lack of coordination and confusion result.

2. Too much is expected too soon. Objectives are set without any real hope of achievement, resulting in disillusionment and the feeling "Just like the old days—promises, promises . . ."

3. No planning for planning is done.

Before any move is made into the planning process, it is imperative that the voluntary organization examine its direction and pace. Direction, from the point of view: Are we moving within the framework of the fundamental issues which concern a voluntary organization? Are our expectations unrealistic? Pace, from the point of view: Are we moving too fast, too soon? Are our expectations unrealistic?

Finally, careful plans must be laid, individuals trained, and data collected for planning. Planning for planning must be carefully done. Remember—planning can be threatening. People must be prepared for planning.

This is not, however, a book on planning. For detailed information, see the Swallow Press publication, *Planning/Marketing for Voluntary Organizations*. It will provide much deeper insight into the entire planning process whereas here we discuss it as a foundation to building an effective board of directors.

In planning for planning, the process must be visual with ends or goals carefully defined. The voluntary sector is besieged with planning models.

Management By Objectives (MBO) has been proved since the 1950s. Program Planning Budget System (PPBS), Program Evaluation and Review Technique (PERT), and Critical Path Method (CPM) networking were the vogue in the 60s. The 70s saw the emergence of zero-based budgeting. Such systems as Key Factor Analysis (KFA) and Management By Result (MBR) were scattered along the way.

The newest vogue—highly visible in the late 70s and now in the 80s—has been marketing. The rising cacophony produced by these systems and their advocates have nearly drowned us in definitions, flowcharts, and procedures.

We badly need to return to basics—one system and one set of definitions. Ask any board of directors and its staff to define a goal, action step, or program and you will receive conflicting definitions.

If we have difficulty in defining the *terms* of planning, it is impossible to describe the *content* of planning.

Our approach is called the *Hierarchy of Planning*; a visual model is depicted in exhibit 10. It has fewer ends: purposes, purpose and action goals, objectives, and targets. Exhibit 11 is a definition of these ends.

Peter F. Drucker has suggested that an organization must be both effective and efficient. Drucker's simple definitions are:

Effective—Doing the *right* things

Efficient—Doing those *things* right

We have added:

Effectiveness
1.   It ought to be done, in one of the three modes:

A. New

B. Old, at same level

C. Old, expanded or reduced

2.   It has a high enough priority to be done.

3.   It has clear and measurable outcomes.

Efficiency
It is being accomplished by the best methods possible at the lowest *practical* cost. This is also known as cost-effectiveness.

Policy—A Definition

Policy, as conventionally defined, refers to broad decisions. In the voluntary sector, we believe the word policy has a more exclusive definition.

It is sometimes forgotten that the first voluntary organizations, as are some today, were *totally* voluntary. Boards decided and also implemented. It is hard for some staff to recognize they came later in the process.

When the first voluntary organization was faced with the necessity of hiring their first staff, the question must have been, "Now who does what?" We believe the answer is effectiveness and efficiency. This first board (not in these terms, of course) said we will keep direct control of effectiveness and delegate efficiency.

Purpose, action goals, and objectives are what makes voluntary organizations effective. Efficiency is accomplished when targets are implemented. Here board policy is effectiveness and includes purpose, action goals, and objectives.

Boards will decide *what* is to be done, but not *how* to do it. Effective decisions require professional input but not professional decisions. The professional's work begins only after a definite course is slated.

Thus, we believe that because of the great variations, policy cannot be defined verbally; it must be *seen*. This requires a hierarchy of planning. Chapter 7 will review policy in detail.

As stated earlier, terminologies vary. If this model and the four

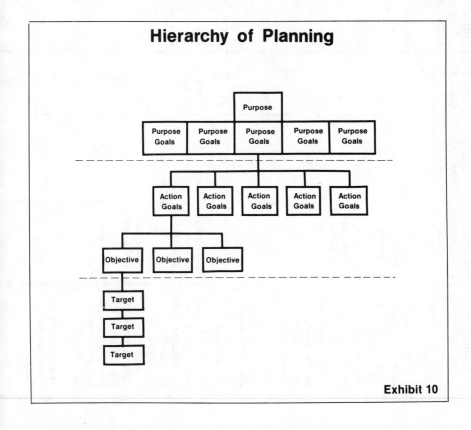

Hierarchy of Planning

Exhibit 10

DEFINITION	IMPORTANT CHARACTERISTICS	WHO FORMULATES (INPUT)	WHO DECIDES	RISK/CONSEQUENCES	RESOLVE COMMITMENT	WHO IS ACCOUNTABLE	DEGREE OF FLEXIBILITY
Purpose The statement which clearly outlines the organizational operating base and philosophy. Purpose goals are expansion of the purpose. Sometimes affects targets. First half of organizational "why".	Believable Desirable Controllable Occasionally Achievable Measurable	Board/ Committee Staff Community Clients	Board Policy	Minimal	None to Minimal	Board Staff chief Executive	These are the philosophical base of the organization. These should be relatively stable and committed so frequent change is not required.
Action Goals Specific outcomes which provide the definitive direction and planning framework. Base for looking into the future, constructing the organization "vision of potentiality". The second half of organizational "why".	Believable Desirable Controllable *Usually* Achievable Measurable Can be sub-divided	Board/ Committee Staff Community Clients	Board Policy	Low	None to Minimal	Board Staff Chief Executive Delegated to Committee Staff	Action goals are strategic planning. These are considerably more flexible than purpose and purpose goals yet should not be subjected to frequent change as this affects objectives and targets. Each action goal should contain a statement of the problem that it

is intended to alleviate.

Objectives Specific outcomes required to achieve a goal. Objectives flow from goals and current issues. They are the key to planning implementation. Two types: *Process*: These last the entire fiscal period. *Event*: These occur at a specific time, then are concluded. This is organizational "what." Objectives provide the base for budget building.	Believable Desirable *Always* Achievable Measurable Controllable Can be subdivided	Board/ Committee Staff Community Clients	Board Policy	Moderate to high	Moderate to high	Board Staff Chief Executive Delegated to Committee Staff	Objectives and targets are tactical planning and should be subjected to frequent scrutiny and evaluation. Targets and objectives are monitored and progress evaluated by the committees and staff to whom the implementation has been assigned.
Targets These are the steps or tasks to be taken to achieve objectives. These are organizational "how" — the "when, where and who" of implementation.	Believable Desirable *Always* Achievable Measurable Controllable	Staff Occasionally Committee	Implementation Principally staff Occasion- ally board	High	High	Board Staff Chief Executive Delegated to Committee Staff	

Exhibit 11

levels are kept in mind, the variety of terms encountered will fit somewhere on the model. To make this point clear, James M. Hardy uses the model and terms illustrated in exhibit 12.[4]

Exhibit 12

Exhibit 10 uses a model different from Dr. Hardy's, and, in three cases, different terms; but the definitions are *exactly* the same.

Dr. Hardy	*This Book*
Ideal Goals	Purpose and Purpose Goals
Operational Goals	Action Goals
Objectives	Objectives
Action Steps	Targets

IMPORTANT NOTE: It is desirable that most objectives be related to action goals. It must be remembered, however, that objectives also flow from current operating issues (see exhibit 13).

This means current operating issues objectives can appear as in exhibit 14.

Many voluntary organizations become split. They have paper purpose and action goals. Objectives and targets do not relate to purpose and action goals. Targets do not relate to objectives. We call this the "funding trap"—going for money rather than for planning.

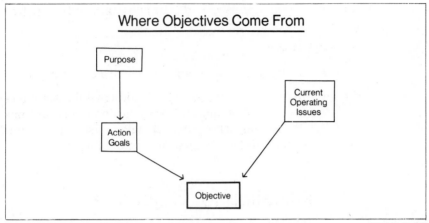

Exhibit 13

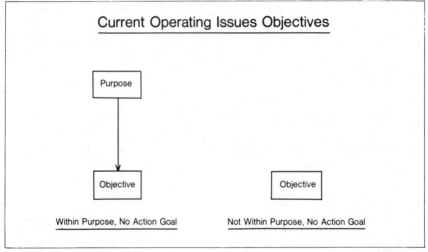

Exhibit 14

Three checks on this issue:

1. If objectives from current operating issues begin to account for 25 percent or more of the total objectives, the planning process needs to be reviewed. When the objectives from current operating issues tend to increase, the organization is moving from a planning stance into problem-solving.

2. As a rule of thumb, objectives without action goals and/or

purposes should be reviewed after two years and one of two decisions should be made:

A. Delete them.

B. Alter or add purpose or action goals to cover them.

3. Finally, we have seen many organizations which are internally congruent (The Hierarchy Holds Together), but externally immaterial. The external data must support the Hierarchy of Planning as illustrated in exhibit 15.

Justification for Objectives

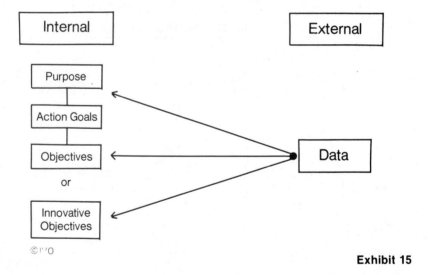

©I'O

Exhibit 15

4. *The Planning Framework*

An organization is managed through the planning process. The planning-management process must be viewed in its totality to be effective. Viewing the process segmentally merely causes confusion and defeats the ends of the process: an effective, self-renewing organization.

If the Hierarchy of Planning is added to the management divisions (process to function) the result is the Planning Framework, the total view. This is illustrated in exhibit 16.

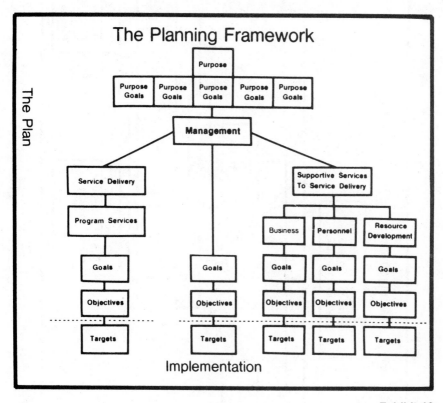

Exhibit 16

If, as we have stated, all but program services are universal then we can say that the action goals and objectives for voluntary organizations are similar. The following seven exhibits show these action goals and objectives. The boxes are blank only in program services. An exception exists in program services—namely, advocacy. We believe every voluntary organization must have an advocacy program both for its clients and for the voluntary concept which is under attack in the United States. (See Voluntary Management Press publication, *Advocacy Programs for Voluntary Organizations.*)

Returning to policy, every action goal and objective noted in exhibits 17-23 is a board policy decision.

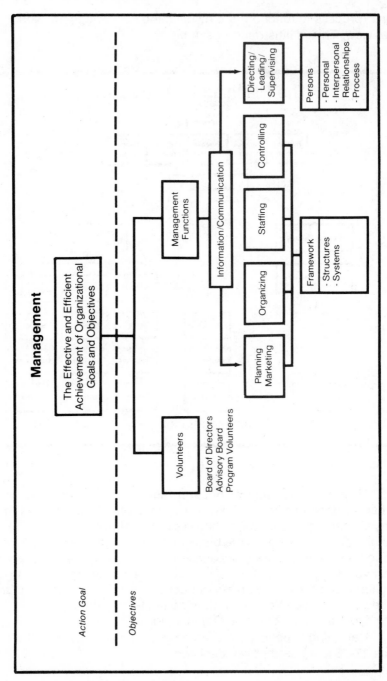

Exhibit 17

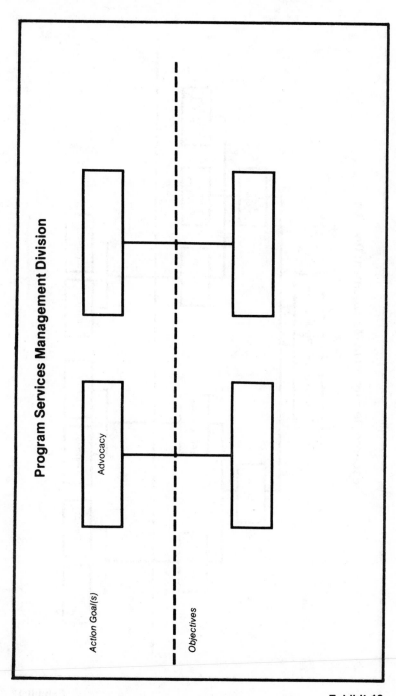

Exhibit 18

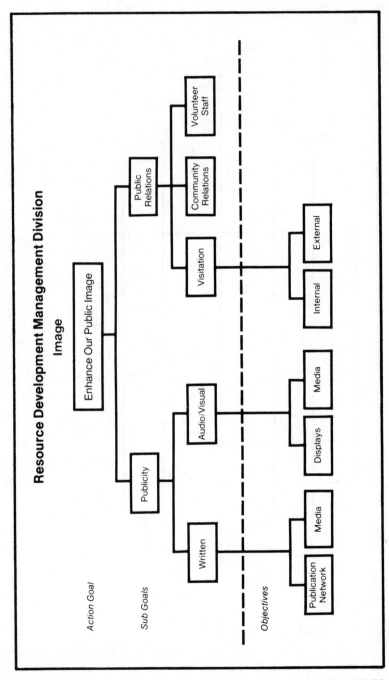

Resource Development Management Division

Image

Action Goal	Enhance Our Public Image
Sub Goals	Publicity / Public Relations
Objectives	Written, Audio/Visual, Visitation, Community Relations, Volunteer Staff — Publication Network, Media, Displays, Media, Internal, External

Exhibit 19

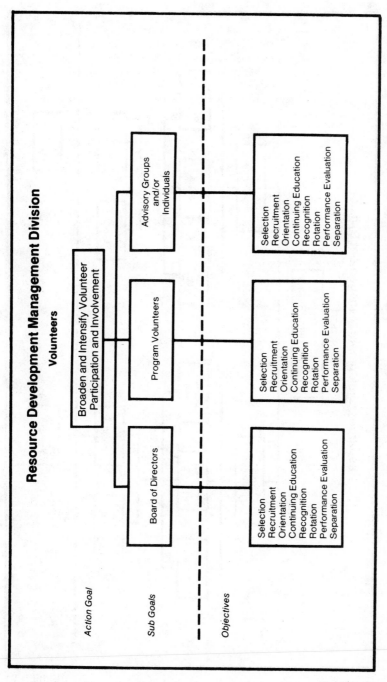

Resource Development Management Division

Volunteers

Action Goal

Broaden and Intensify Volunteer Participation and Involvement

Sub Goals

Board of Directors

Program Volunteers

Advisory Groups and/or Individuals

Objectives

Selection
Recruitment
Orientation
Continuing Education
Recognition
Rotation
Performance Evaluation
Separation

Selection
Recruitment
Orientation
Continuing Education
Recognition
Rotation
Performance Evaluation
Separation

Selection
Recruitment
Orientation
Continuing Education
Recognition
Rotation
Performance Evaluation
Separation

Exhibit 20

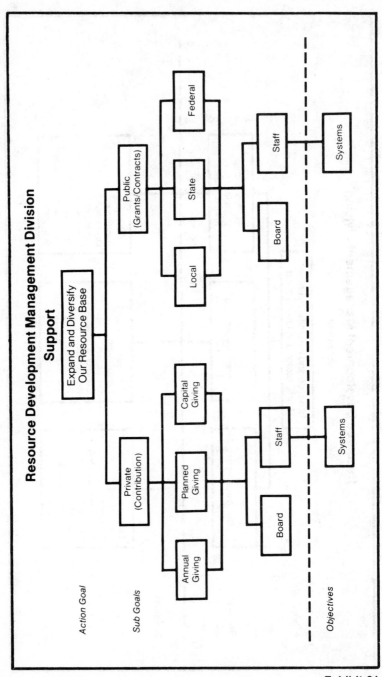

Resource Development Management Division Support

Action Goal

Sub Goals

Objectives

Expand and Diversify Our Resource Base

Public (Grants/Contracts)

Federal

State

Local

Staff

Board

Systems

Private (Contribution)

Capital Giving

Planned Giving

Annual Giving

Staff

Board

Systems

Exhibit 21

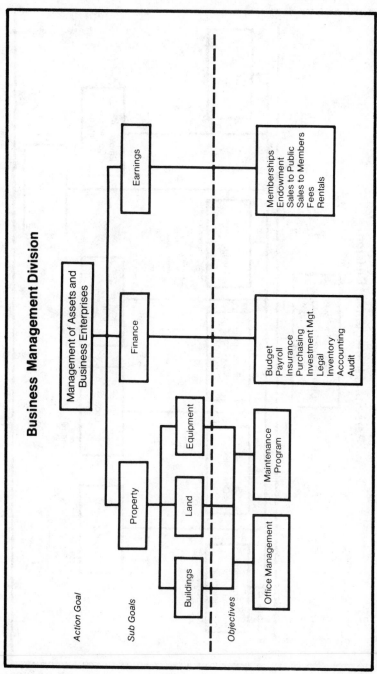

Exhibit 22

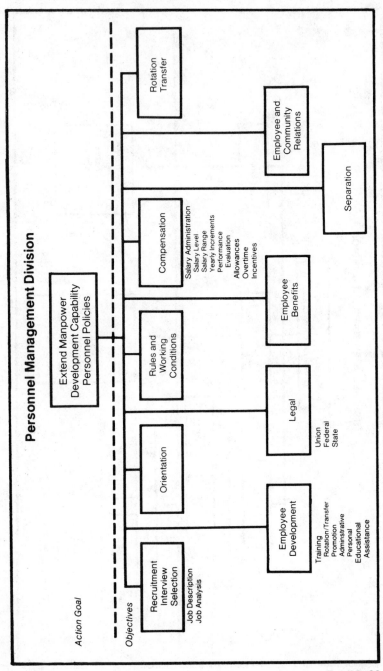

Personnel Management Division

Action Goal

Extend Manpower
Development Capability
Personnel Policies

Objectives

Recruitment
Interview
Selection

Job Description
Job Analysis

Orientation

Rules and
Working
Conditions

Compensation

Salary Administration
Salary Level
Salary Range
Yearly Increments
Performance
Evaluation
Allowances
Overtime
Incentives

Rotation
Transfer

Employee and
Community
Relations

Separation

Employee
Benefits

Legal

Union
Federal
State

Employee
Development

Training
Rotation/Transfer
Promotion
Administrative
Personal
Educational
Assistance

Exhibit 23

To repeat, the purpose of this chapter is not to define the planning process, but to supply a few frameworks within which planning can begin. Further, the aim is to impress upon the reader that boards can be effective—truly effective—only within a basic concept of management understood and agreed upon by the board of directors and its staff. Boards are effective in direct proportion to the effectiveness of the planning process within the voluntary organization.

Finally, earlier in this chapter it was stated that one of the two greatest roadblocks to planning in voluntary organizations is restricting it to program services. We close with a discussion of the second of the two great roadblocks to planning: forgetting that planning is basically *people*. Institutions are only people. We must learn how to help people deal with change (because that is what planning is— change) by reducing the anxiety that flows from it. We call upon Gardner again to put the "people factor" of planning in perspective:

> Unless we attend to the requirements of renewal, aging institutions and organizations will bring our civilization to moldering ruin. Unless we cope with the ways in which modern society oppresses the individual, we shall lose the creative spark that renews both societies and men. Unless we foster versatile, innovative and self-renewing men and women, all the ingenious social arrangements in the world will not help us.[5]

A word must be said about structure and freedom. A common complaint is that structures are rigid, forcing people into creativity-killing levels and boxes.

This does not necessarily need to be. Intellectuals may attack organizations and structures as being anti-freedom. It would be useful, however, to remember that freedom comes *only* with structure. The problem is that our attempts to provide "freedom with structure" too often result in rigidity—a reduction of freedom. Freedom and structure should be considered interdependent, not mutually exclusive.

Finally, in the planning task, we must recognize that change is an inevitable by-product. Change is always a threat to somebody's security. It behooves us to look as closely at what planning will do *to the people within the organization* as we do at what planning will do *for our constituency*. In other words, we must carefully plan the planning task.

Let's not wind up as one executive did: "The planning process and the resultant plan were excellent. The problem was we never did find a way to implement the plan." We must know about people.

Method [planning] goes far to prevent trouble; for it makes the task easy, hinders confusion, saves abundance of time, and instructs those who have business pending, what to do and what to hope.

William Penn

NOTES

1. Gardner, *Self-Renewal*, p. 3.
2. James Hilton, *Lost Horizon* (New York: William Morrow & Co., 1971), p. 197. edition) p. 197.
3. Peter F. Drucker, *The Practice of Management* (New York: Harper & Row, 1954), p. 15.
4. James M. Hardy, *Corporate Planning for Nonprofit Organizations*, p. 1.
5. Gardner, *Self-Renewal*, p. 14.

THE ORGANIZATION OF THE BOARD OF DIRECTORS AND BOARD/STAFF RELATIONSHIPS

5

Definitions of an organization (as in planning) number as many as there are those who attempt to define it. Ours is rather simple:

A group or groups working together within a framework to do something, held together by an information/communication network.

Let us examine this definition:

A group or groups working together

The key groups in a voluntary organization are its board of directors and its staff.

Within a framework

By nature, humans must understand their places, the relationship of those places, and the definition of roles. John W. Gardner has said (in *Self-Renewal*):

In the ever renewing society, what matters is a system or framework within which continuous innovation, renewal and rebirth can occur.[1]

— A basic purpose of this book.

To do something

The planning framework is the "doing." The role of management

Management Divisions to Standing Committees

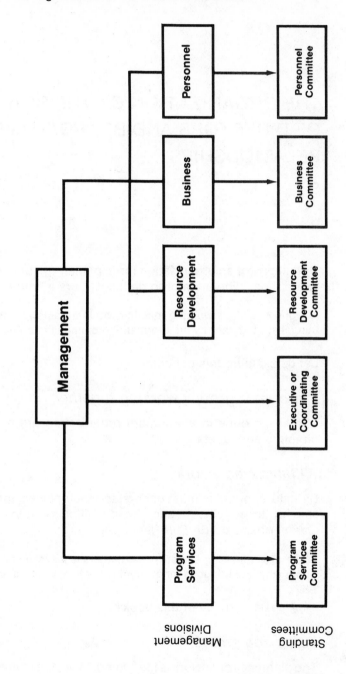

Exhibit 24

is to assure that organizational outcomes are effective and efficient.

Held together by an information/communication network

Without information and a communications network to route information, nothing happens.

Part of the framework is board organization. There is an old management truism—"Form Follows Function." The management divisions serve as the form or basis for a board committee's structure. The staff are hired to manage and implement the management divisions. A board must be organized in the same way. The standing committees of the board should correspond to the management divisions (exhibit 24). The formal board organization is shown in exhibit 25.

Three notes:

1. The committee's job is found in the planning framework. See chapter 6 for greater detail and appendix 2.

2. Board organization depends upon the complexity of the organization. Some organizations are small enough that the board acts as a committee of the whole. Some boards have only two or three committees. The planning framework is the key for committee formulation. This describes the complexity of the organization.

3. Beware of the executive committee! Executive committees still become detriments, although great concern exists about their function and usefulness. Much more efficient decision-making involves only a small group. As the influence of the executive committee increases, the influence of the board as a whole decreases. The first place to look for a problem when the cry is heard "They (meaning the board) never do anything" is to look at the executive committee.

   Executive committees have legal standing, and can commit the entire board to a course of action. The entire board becomes responsible for what the executive committee does.

   We feel that geographically contiguous organizations

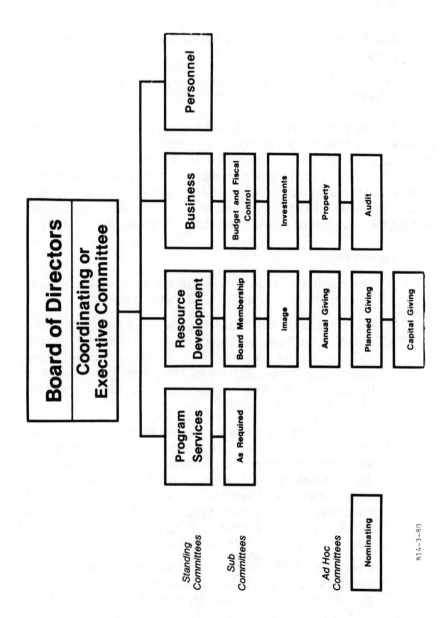

Exhibit 25

should consider abolishing the executive committee. Little need exists for this group to take an action that the entire board cannot be brought together to consider.

Executive committees often act as screeners or checkers on committee reports to go before the board. This is an enormous waste of time. If agenda building is properly done, a committee should report directly to the board, not to the executive committee first.

In place of the executive committee, we recommend looking at a coordinating committee. The exception is in geographically spread organizations. National or regional boards will require an executive committee to conduct their business. Exhibit 26 gives some considerations for executive and coordinating committees.

In voluntary organizations where there are two or more staff, the board-volunteer/staff relationships must be clear. Basically, the only staff member who is directly responsible to board volunteers is the staff chief executive. Subordinate staff relate to committees and to committee chairpersons; but they are not accountable to them. Exhibit 27 illustrates this concept. The solid lines are lines of authority, and the dotted lines represent feedback, communication, consultation, and advisory relationships. We call it the basic management square.

The board of directors has final responsibility for the achievement of the organization's goals and objectives. To accomplish this task it takes an executive director to implement board policy and organize itself to establish that policy, to fulfill its role, and to provide support to the staff. Exhibit 28 has added additional persons to the Basic Management Square.

After the board has decided its committee structure and hired the staff chief executive, the board elects a chairperson or president. The following takes place:

1. The staff chief executive designates which staff members will be responsible to work with the committee.

2. The chairperson or president selects his or her committee chairpersons and recruits them by visiting them in their place of business, home or wherever convenient for the prospect. The staff person responsible for the committee

COORDINATING COMMITTEE
and EXECUTIVE COMMITTEE

Coordinating Committee

Functions:

1. Coordinates and supervises the planning/budgeting process.

2. Prepares for the board of directors the performance evaluation (which includes salary and release recommendations) of the staff chief executive officer.

Executive Committee

Possible Composition:

CHAIRPERSON OF BOARD

PRESIDENT OF BOARD

(If there is no chairperson or if there is a chairperson *and* a president of the board)

(The chairperson of the executive committee is the chief board officer, either chairperson or president. In some cases where a chairperson and a president exist, the president may act as the chairperson of the executive committee.)

EXECUTIVE VICE-CHAIRPERSON or EXECUTIVE VICE-PRESIDENT

(Where a chairperson *or* a president is the chief board officer, this position is sometimes the chairperson or president designate.)

VICE-CHAIRPERSON (OR VICE-PRESIDENT) FOR PROGRAM SERVICES*

VICE-CHAIRPERSON (OR VICE-PRESIDENT) FOR BUSINESS*

VICE-CHAIRPERSON (OR VICE-PRESIDENT) FOR PERSONNEL*

VICE-CHAIRPERSON (OR VICE-PRESIDENT) FOR RESOURCE DEVELOPMENT*

SECRETARY (and, if desired, ASSISTANT SECRETARY)

TWO AT-LARGE MEMBERS (appointed or elected)

IMMEDIATE PAST CHAIRPERSON OR PRESIDENT

*All vice-chairpersons or vice-presidents are also chairpersons of standing committees.

All members of either committee should be board volunteers.

Exhibit 26

should also accompany the chairperson or president. This will solidify the relationship. The staff chief executive need not join them.

3. The relationship between the chairperson and staff chief executive is shown by a dotted line. The staff chief executive reports to the board, not to the chairperson or president. This is an important relationship. (See the Voluntary Management Press publication, "The Chairperson of the Board and the Executive Director—A Critical Relationship.")

BOARD - STAFF RELATIONSHIPS
THE BASIC MANAGEMENT SQUARE

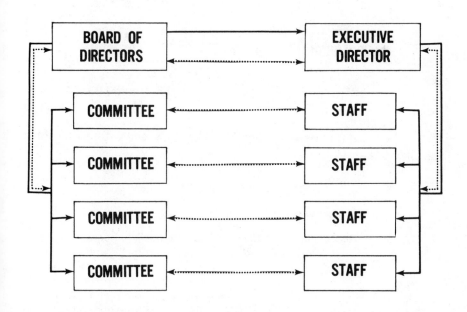

Exhibit 27

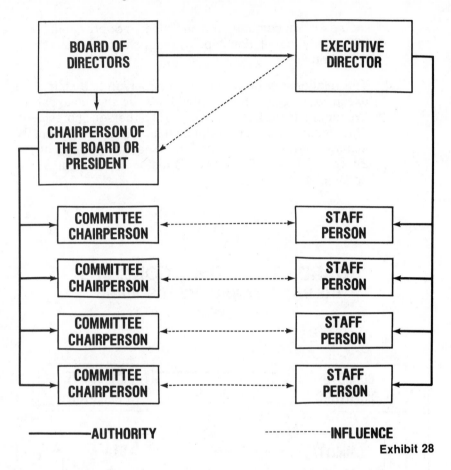

Exhibit 28

Exhibit 29 illustrates accountability and where to go to solve problems that will develop.

PROBLEM	RESOLUTION
1. Committee chairperson dissatisfied with individual staff.	1. Committee chairperson discusses problem with board chairperson. The committee chairperson then contacts the executive director. Sometimes chairperson will accompany to resolve issue.

2. Individual staff member dissatisfied with committee chairperson.

2. Individual staff member discusses problem with executive director. Both go to chairperson to resolve problem.

3. Sub-committee chairperson dissatisfied with the individual staff person.

3. The sub-committee chairperson consults with committee chairperson, then with the staff person. If problem can't be handled at that end, person moves on to step 1.

4. Staff person dissatisfied with sub-committee chairperson.

4. The staff person consults with committee chairperson. If problem can't be resolved at this end, person moves to step 2.

5. Chairperson and/or executive director dissatisfied with the others.

5. The issue is resolved at the board of directors level.

Accountability and Problem Solving

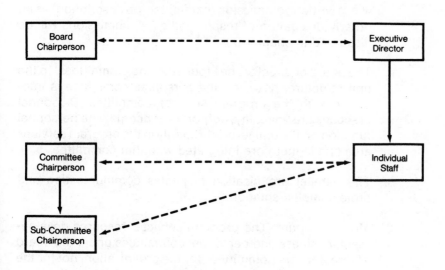

Exhibit 29

A useful publication is "So You Are Now A Chairperson" from Voluntary Management Press. This publication goes into greater detail on the board chairperson's leadership team, board officer, and his/her relationship with the staff chief executive.

There are some voluntary organizations which have several units, each of which has a board.

Exhibits 30 and 31 show the relationships in a multi-unit voluntary organization and are based on exhibits 27, 28, and 29.

1. The board of directors is the legal body vested with responsibility for operating the corporation in accordance with state laws, as designated in the corporate constitution and bylaws.

2. The management of individual unit operations is delegated to boards of managers. The specifics of this delegated responsibility and authority are clearly stated in the board of managers' bylaws (Appendix I) which is the effective commission to the board of managers to act on behalf of the board of directors as specified therein.

3. The board of managers organizes itself through an appropriate committee structure and presents each committee with a written commission (committee job description) as an orderly delegation of responsibility. (Commissions will be discussed in chapter 6.)

4. The board of directors has four standing committees. In the unit structure, however, the personnel committee is integrated with the program services committee. Personnel practices are, in reality, corporate concerns. The personnel function on the unit level is primarily in the program services area and is therefore integrated with that committee.

5. The parallel organization facilitates communication and project implementation.

6. Most important: The program services, resource development, business and personnel committees under the board of directors are committees for the organization, not for the board alone. Policy recommendations for board action come through these committees.

Periodically, the chairperson of the corporate standing committees should meet with their counterpart chairpersons on the board of managers' level for feedback, communications, advice, consultation, and training.

Exhibit 30 brings together the lines of authority applying the principles illustrated in exhibit 31. The only staff member who is directly responsible to the board, or to any individual board volunteer, is the executive director. Members of the administrative staff are responsible to their committee chairpersons and committees on a "dotted-line" basis. The unit directors are not responsible to their boards; they are responsible to the executive director.

If conflict arises, conflict resolution moves up the two sides of the organization. If the executive director cannot resolve the conflict between a unit board of managers and the unit director, the board of directors becomes responsible for effecting a resolution. (Legal authority for this resides in the bylaws, samples of which are found in appendix I.)

In the governance of the Newport Organization, the chairperson of the board of managers is represented on the board of directors and on the executive committee, ensuring that the voice of the units will be heard officially. As was stated previously, the chairpersons of the standing committees of the board of directors meet periodically with their counterpart chairpersons of the board of managers, thus maintaining a high level of communication between the corporation and its units.

Here, the concept is that the board volunteer/staff relationship must be based on a clear recognition, understanding and acceptance of the distinctive board and staff roles. One point of all this apparatus is that organizations be governed through board policy. Chapter 7 will discuss the board policy process.

To conclude, board and staff organizations should be parallel with staff and board relating at the committee level, regardless of how organizations are put together—as noted below (from Gardner, *Self-Renewal*, p. 5.):

> Organizations are "organic"—an arrangement of people and resources for the achievement of defined goals and objectives. Management should organize and mobilize resources to achieve these goals and objectives.
> There are two primary schools of thought relative to the structures which have been constructed to facilitate mobilization. Traditional hierarchies—with their definite superior-subordinate structure—are,

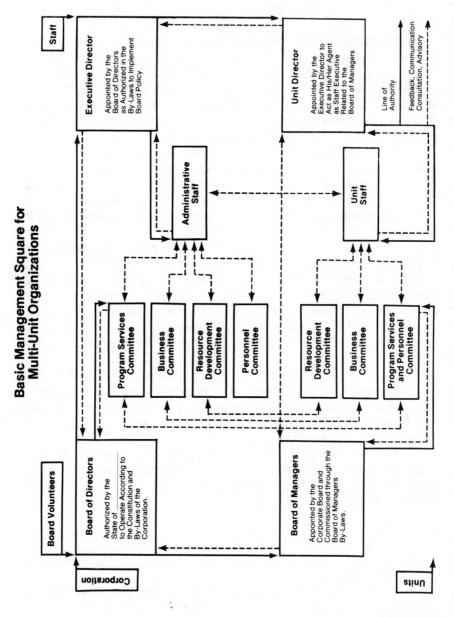

Basic Management Square for Multi-Unit Organizations

Staff

Executive Director

Appointed by the Board of Directors as Authorized in the By-Laws to Implement Board Policy.

Unit Director

Appointed by the Executive Director to Act as His/Her Agent as Staff Executive Related to the Board of Managers

Line of Authority

Feedback, Communication Consultation, Advisory

Administrative Staff

Unit Staff

Program Services Committee

Business Committee

Resource Development Committee

Personnel Committee

Resource Development Committee

Business Committee

Program Services and Personnel Committee

Board Volunteers

Board of Directors

Authorized by the State of to Operate According to the Constitution and By-Laws of the Corporation.

Board of Managers

Appointed by the Corporate Board and Commissioned through the Board of Managers By-Laws.

Corporation

Units

Exhibit 30

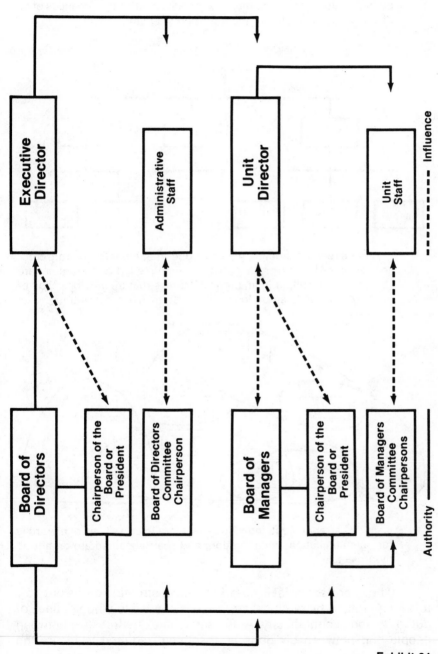

Exhibit 31

by their nature, unable to meet the creative and changing needs of individuals, as illustrated in the following diagram:

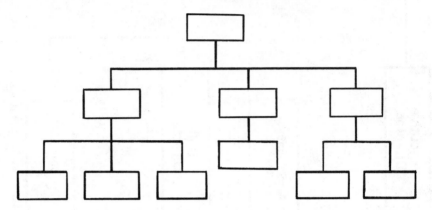

A more recent school of thought argues that organizations are composed of inter-locking groups which are disrupted when hierarchies are constructed, resulting in an organizational structure that looks something like this and can be loosely called a matrix organization.

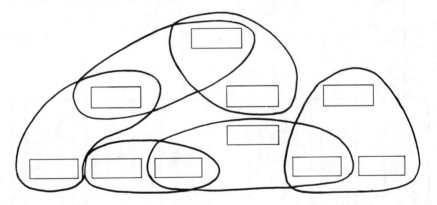

In this arrangement, individuals feel free to cross lines of hierarchy for communication, collaboration, and assistance and are organized by project.

The important point is not what kind of structure exists but how it is to operate. A hierarchical structure is needed to pinpoint lines of authority and accountability. At the same time, the free flow between people and between divisions is absolutely required to insure the achievement of goals and objectives and to provide the basis for renewal. The existence of this free flow directly relates to the management style of the chairperson of the board and the staff chief executive. Their job becomes one of building a strong sense of group achievement rather than obedience to orders. Authority becomes subordinate to support and encouragement; creativity and experimentation replace "doing it by the book." The organization then takes on a shape something like this:

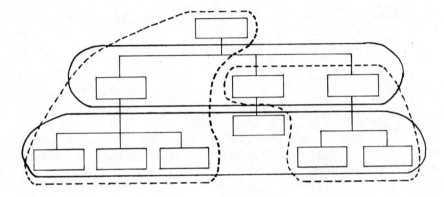

THE ROLE AND FUNCTION OF COMMITTEES

6

"The Task Force of Democracy!" "Our democratic society could not function without them." These are high words of praise—clear indications of the critical role of committees. And yet in every comedian's book of favorite jokes there is at least one about committees: "A camel is a horse put together by a committee." Clever speakers feel they must join the attack: "A committee is a group of the unfit trying to lead the unwilling to do the unnecessary." Board members snicker: "What committee did they stick you on?" Staff executives gripe: "I've got another committee meeting coming up. What am I going to do with it?" And finally, the fear of anyone who is part of an organization: "Don't make a suggestion—you'll be appointed chairperson of a committee to look into it."

The paradox is obvious, the implications rather frightening. The truth of the matter is that when we say our board is not functioning, we really mean our committees are not functioning. The effectiveness of a board is measured by its committees, not the board itself; for it is at the committee level that a board will succeed or fail. Every board volunteer must be effectively involved at the committee level where the real work, the debates, and the interaction take place. When a committee recommendation comes before the board, the recommendation should already have had a thorough screening at the committee level. The board can then take such action as it deems advisable on the reports and recommendations of the committee. A committee need not put together a camel instead of a horse!

Functioning

A successfully functioning committee must have these in-gredients:

1. *A specific commission.* This is a definitive document which describes clearly what the committee is to do, per-mitting the committee members to answer the question: "To what extent do we understand what we are to do and why we are to do it?"

2. *An effective chairperson.* The key to an effective com-mittee is an effective chairperson. He/she is the one who sets the tone, pace, and strategies for the committee. He/she must be thoroughly acquainted with the goals of the organi-zation and the part the committee plays in the achievement of these goals. He/she delegates and coordinates work and provides a climate in which thoughtful deliberation is pos-sible. He is quite the "leader-enabler."

3. *An effective staff.* If the key to an effective committee is an effective chairperson, the key to an effective chairperson is an effective staff executive. He/she must work closely with the chairperson, assisting in the preparation of agendas and providing all the pertinent data required to operate an effec-tive committee meeting.

4. *Effective committee meetings.* If the first three ingredients are present, a good committee meeting generally results. Such meetings are action-oriented, based on a sound agenda, with all necessary data available for the decisions to be made. The Swallow Press publication, "Condensed Parliamentary Procedures" based on Roberts Rules of Or-der is useful here.

5. *Committee members thoughtfully appointed.* Committee members should be appointed with a clear view of the goals the committee must achieve and of the skills brought by each committee member to assist in the achievement of those goals.

In the appointment of committee members, it is important to note that committee membership does not necessarily require board membership. Committees could well include people with specific skills who would perform important consultative functions. Construction people, for example, could serve on the property committee, advertising people on the public relations committee, educators on the program services committee, and so on. These possibilities should not be ignored.

In fact, we advocate that when a new board volunteer is recruited that he/she be told the committee assignment at that time. A new board member will be more effective more quickly serving on a committee that falls within his/her vocation, avocation, or hobby. After at least one year of service, a new board volunteer should be able to serve on any committee of his/her choice.

Executives fear the loss of control and communication if they allow staff to work with committees. This can be avoided by the agenda building process and meeting review as shown in exhibit 32. Exhibit 33 shows a sample business committee agenda. Exhibit 34 outlines a format reviewing an item on the agenda. This should be mailed in advance. Exhibit 35 lists a sample program services committee agenda. Exhibit 36 shows a format similar to that in exhibit 34.

The *Hillsdale College Leadership Letter* published the following very sound suggestions for handling volunteer committees:

1. The governing board must know the aims of the organization and agree to the importance of a sound committee structure to reach them.

2. This group must understand the need for each committee and agree to its function, role, and its relationship to other committees.

3. To assure an objective and a balanced judgment representative of the total group, the president should not appoint a committee without consulting his board—except in case of emergency.

4. The board should carefully consider the purpose of the committee in question and select members who are best fitted to advance that purpose.

5. A potential member should have his position dignified by an interview before his appointment is confirmed. He should know that his unique knowledge and skills make him important to the total group. He should learn some-

thing of the other members who will share the responsibility with him.

6.   The board should select a committee chairperson with care and make clear the importance of his/her job and its objectives before he/she is appointed.

7.   After the appointment, the president should convene the committee briefly to make clear the baselines within which the chairperson of the committee must direct the group.

8.   The president of the organization should be responsible for making certain that the committee meets and moves to complete its assignment.

9.   The president should meet with the chairperson or with the whole committee to be sure that it has reached its goal and will give a report to bring credit to its work.

10.   If the committee completes its assignment, a commendation for its good work and the results should be given and the committee disbanded.[1]

Minutes

Minutes are an important part of committee work but are seldom well done—if done at all. Minutes should be kept, however, as they are the reference material for any questions which may arise about committee actions.

1.   Since the person who takes minutes does not have an opportunity to participate fully, a competent staff secretary should be assigned to that task.

2.   A draft of the minutes should be reviewed by the responsible staff person and approved by the board or committee secretaries before the minutes are distributed.

3.   Minutes should be distributed within a week of the meeting.

4.   Minutes should be concise and complete.

5.   Committee reports should be presented in writing to assure accurate reporting.

6.   Each person who makes a motion should jot down his own wording for the benefit of exact recording.

In summary, there should be a set format for minutes. It should correspond to the agenda. In reality, only two things take place in committee or board meetings. Yet, both should be either included in the minutes or attached to it:

Communication—the passing on of helpful information

Decisions—deciding to do something

If the item is communication, it should be attached to the

Committee Agenda Building and Meeting Review

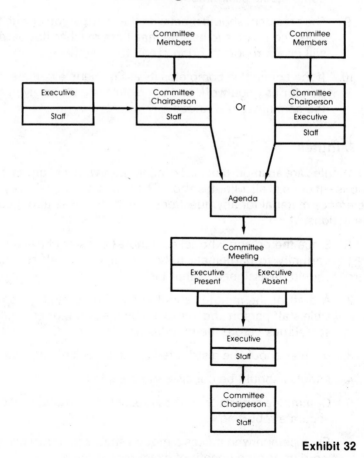

Exhibit 32

NEWPORT ORGANIZATION

BUSINESS COMMITTEE MEETING

April 10, 19_

A G E N D A

1. Approval of Agenda

2. Newport Organization Accounting Proposal

3. Review Investment of Current Bequests

4. Future Investments of Endowment Fund

5. Review of Current Cash Position and Cash-Flow Problem in June

6. Other Business

7. Adjournment

ATTENDING:

George L. Pierce, Chairman
Thomas F. Adams
Herman L. Dent
Harold P. Jefferson
Sylvia N. Otterness
Frank Prett
Carleton S. Rhodes

Samuel L. Black
Executive Director

Herbert R. Munsey
Director of Business Administration

Jane L. Pryor
Associate Director
   of Business Administration

Exhibit 33

NEWPORT ORGANIZATION

BUSINESS COMMITTEE MEETING

April 10, 19__

AGENDA ITEM # 2

Situation:

Beginning July 1, 19__, all reporting is to be based on cost accounting principles, requiring all items of income and expense to be classified into programs and activities with their related statistics. At present, our system does not provide for the collection of this data.

Blodgett & Co. was engaged to design a system for the collection and reporting of this information in order to satisfy the new requirements as well as to provide a management tool for internal control. This system was presented to our computer firm for a peliminary estimate of the costs of developing and operating the system on an annual basis. Their proposal is attached.

Conversion costs from the present system, for both fund accounting and payroll function, will be approximately $5,000, bringing the total set-up costs to around $27,400. Monthly payroll processing under the new system will be around $500 per month, or $6,000 per year, bringing the total annual operating costs to approximately $34,200. These costs are based on estimates, since the volume of transactions under the new system was unknown.

Options:

Based on the above information, several options are available:

1.   Implement entire system with full operation beginning July 1, 19__ .

Exhibit 34a

2. Implement entire system, but omit budget in-
    put, resulting in reports containing actual fig-
    ures only. This would delete the control factor
    and leave interpretation of results questionable.

3. Delay implementation of system. This would
    require the hiring of *at least* two additional staff
    persons in order to gather and formulate man-
    ually the data necessary for Community Fund
    reporting.

Recommendation: It is the belief of the Administrative staff that this
system, while providing the necessary information
for reporting, will also serve as a tool for internal
control in analyzing the cost effectiveness and organizational equity of all programs, and we recommend that the Committee approve the proposal as
outlined in Option #1.

Action Required: Review the proposal and available options, and
make a recommendation to the Board of Directors.

Exhibit 34b

NEWPORT ORGANIZATION

UNIT 1

PROGRAM SERVICES COMMITTEE

April 17, 19___

Lester B. Cannon, Chairperson
Presiding

A G E N D A

1. Approval of Agenda
2. Program Services Report   William H. Logan
3. Review of Statistics   William H. Logan
4. Request for Individual Tutoring Juanita Perez, Chairperson
                                     Education Sub-Committee
5. Progress Report on Teen Center   Herman L. Dent, Chairperson
                                     Social and Recreational
                                     Sub-Committee
6. Review of 19___ Budget Process   Herbert L. Munsey
    and Role of Program Services
    Committee
7. Other Business
8. Adjournment

ATTENDING:

Lester B. Cannon, Chairperson   William H. Logan, Program
                                       Director
Franklin Byman
Gordon Fletcher   Louis Bend, Group Work
                                       Supervisor
Juanita Perez
Clifton Rhodes   Herbert L. Munsey, Director
Mary Wilson   Business Administration

Exhibit 35

NEWPORT ORGANIZATION

UNIT 1

PROGRAM SERVICES COMMITTEE MEETING

April 17, 19___

AGENDA ITEM #4

Situation:

In the last six months there has been an increasing number of requests from parents to help their children with specific school-
subject problems. The staff has discussed the problem with the three
elementary school principals and with the high school principal, who
have confirmed that the individual tutoring requirements of students
have begun to outstrip the capability of the schools to deal with the
problem.

The major factor is that the student turnover-rate in the schools has
reached 50 percent. The area has become highly transient. There is
a need for the Newport Organization to move into a modified tutoring program.

Program Requirements:

The areas in which most help is needed are reading, mathematics,
algebra, basic English, Spanish and plane geometry.

We estimate that there is a total of 48 members in these categories,
as follows:

Reading—15	Algebra—9	Spanish—4
Mathematics—7	English—10	Plane Geometry—3

The schools will share textbooks with us and materials for individual
student needs. We have also established a tentative system for reporting back to school.

The tutors would be nearby Franklin College students, school
teachers, and high school seniors. These people would be volunteers.

This program would fall under the leadership of Mr. Bend.

We have the room-space available for the program. We estimate costs
at $25 per month for materials. We have this amount in the budget.

Recommendations:

The program staff would like to institute the program on a three-
month trial basis. At the end of the three months, the staff would report to the Education Subcommittee, which supports the recommendation.

Action Required by Program Services Committee:

If the Program Committee approves the program, the program must
be submitted to the Board of Directors or the Executive Committee. This is a policy decision.

Exhibit 36

NEWPORT ORGANIZATION

PROGRAM SERVICES COMMITTEE MEETING

April 17, 19__

MINUTES

ATTENDING:

Lester B. Cannon, Chairperson	William H. Logan, Program
Franklin Byman	Director
Gordon Fletcher	Louis Bend, Group Work
Juanita Perez	Supervisor
Clifton Rhodes	Herbert L. Munsey, Director
Mary Wilson	Business Administration

Agenda Item	Communication Attached	DECISION		
		Decision	Responsi-bility for follow-up	Deadline
2. Program Service Report	X			
3. Review of Statistics	X			
4. Request for individual tutoring		yes—6 no—0	W.H. Logan	Report progress in one month
5. Progress report on Teen Center	X			
6. Review of 19__ budget process and role of Program Services Committee	X			

Exhibit 37

minutes, not integrated into the minutes. If the item is decision, only three things need be reported:

The decision made

The responsibility assigned for follow-up

The deadlines for action

A review of discussions is futile, as they are difficult to write and time-consuming to read, and add little value to the decision made. Exhibit 37 is a minutes format attached to the full minute write-up. This provides a simple way to look up actions of previous meetings. These formats apply to board meetings, as well.

Committee Commissions

"May I see the job description?" is probably one of the first requests made by a staff executive when interviewing for a new position. It is absolutely necessary if he/she is going to understand the requirements of the position. Curiously, the staff often asks board volunteers to accept responsibilities without giving them any clear definition of the requirements. Committees, too, may be asked to function without any explanation of what is expected of them. Just as the staff requires job descriptions, so do committees. Committee job descriptions—known as "commissions"—should have three basic components:

General Commission:	A broad statement of the purpose of the committee.
Appointments and Composition:	How appointments are made and who serves on each committee.
Responsibilities:	A definite description of the activities required of the committee.

(Sample committee commissions are in Appendix II.)

Manuals of Operation

Manuals of operation are constructed to assist a committee in the accomplishment of its tasks. They contain procedures and forms which are useful to both board members and staff. (Sample manual of operation may be found in Appendix III.)

Ad-hoc Committees

Ad-hoc committees are short duration committees formed to accomplish a specific task. There must be a clear differentiation between ad-hoc and standing committees:

1. Standing committees deal with the *ongoing processes* of an organization. They are concerned with system maintenance and evaluation.

2. Ad-hoc committees are formed to accomplish specific tasks such as research, study, evaluation, or problem-solving. Some special considerations for ad-hoc committees are:

    A. They should be of predetermined duration.

    B. They can be formed either from within a specific committee or from any or all of the committees of the board.

    C. They can elicit participation from outside the board and committee structure of the organization.

    D. They should have a clear commission outlining what they should accomplish.

As stated before, a committee need not be composed only of board volunteers. Many boards increase involvement through non-board members on committees. Many boards require that the committee chairpersons be board volunteers. It really doesn't matter.

A caution—if a person is asked to serve on a committee, let him/her vote, board member or not. Some organizations give the vote only to board volunteers. If a vote is not to be given, make those individuals advisors. In exhibit 38, the solid lines indicate accountabilities while the dotted lines show the consultive relationship.

Role of Committees

With all this, what does a committee really do? Its work is derived from the planning framework.

1. It recommends new items or changes to the action goals and objectives under its jurisdiction to the board of directors.

2. It monitors the result of the action goals and objectives when approved by the board of directors.

Committee Composition

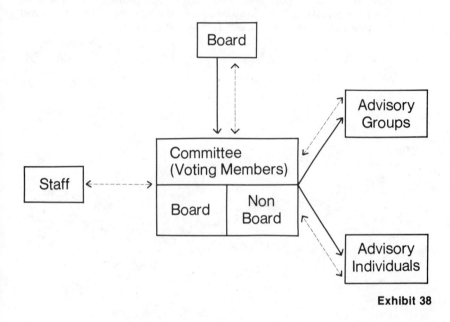

Exhibit 38

3. It coordinates its activities with the other committees through the coordinating or executive committee.

A well-known industrialist once said this of committees: "If you want to kill any idea in the world today, get a committee working on it." In contrast, someone at a recent conference spoke expansively of the value of committees, claiming that all organizational ills would be reduced to mere minor nuisances if only we were to operationalize committees. The ideal, of course, lies somewhere in between these two extremes. Committees are vital to the work of voluntary organizations; they are the basic action elements of voluntarism.

A final point about committees. Many organizations use committees as a training ground for new board volunteers. These organizations fill board openings from committee members. In these organizations, individuals cannot be elected to the board of directors unless they have served well as a committee member.

NOTES

1. "The Care and Feeding of Committees," the *Hillsdale College Leadership Letter*, Vol. II, No. 7, December, 1963. All copyright privileges are now in the names of Kolivosky & Taylor and the publication is published under the name of K-T Notes, available from Box 292, Hillsdale, Michigan.

THE BOARD POLICY PROCESS
7

Unfortunately, the policy determination of voluntary boards of directors is summed up in these words of a staff executive: "My board doesn't make policy—I do. They don't know enough to really be able to help me in my job. What they do, in effect, is simply ratify *my* policy." The effective board-policy role is summed up very well by Melvin E. Sims, president of FS Services, Inc., in a speech entitled: "Management–Board Relations, A Board President's View" (Graduate Institute of Cooperative Leadership; Columbia, Missouri; July 25, 1973). Mr. Sims said:

> Regardless of the chief executive officer's attitude concerning the importance of, or the competency of, the board of directors, it is prudent to remember that the board has the legal authority to impose its will. The manager who views his board as an unnecessary nuisance flirts with disaster, both for his own future career and for the future of the cooperative. Sooner or later, a director will read the articles of incorporation and the bylaws and fully comprehend the powers vested in the board.

Although this statement was delivered to a group of businessmen, the concept embodied in it also reflects the reality of the situation in voluntary organizations. Further on in his speech, Mr. Sims made some critically important comments with respect to policy considerations:

> Although it does not appear in the job description of many chief executive officers, he has a significant responsibility in the area of training and development of the board of directors. He spends more time with the board, as a group, than any other person and has a unique op-

77

portunity to teach by supervising actual experiences. If a member of the board gets into operating activities, the manager should make him aware of the division of responsibility if the chairperson fails to do so. Obviously, the manager must know the difference between operating and policy questions. Generally speaking, if it is a matter of what is to be done or where the cooperative is to go, it probably lies in the policy area. If, on the other hand, it is a question of how the work is to be done or who is to do it, it probably lies in the operating area and should be a decision of the manager.

The manager should have an active part in policy development. He is close to the problems and has staff available to assist in doing research. Broad policy determination, however, is clearly a policy decision to be made by the board. For instance, the basic objective of the cooperative is a fundamental decision for the board to make.

I feel strongly that the manager should present his recommendations in writing. Each recommendation should be presented in a brief and concise statement following a commentary which enumerates the alternatives and the advantages and disadvantages of the proposition. A written statement is generally more carefully researched, more clearly stated, and more easily understood—and it becomes a matter of record. A sensitive manager, who really knows his board, should be able to generally predict how every director will react to a given recommendation. He should be able to anticipate almost every question and have an accurate, complete answer—either in the commentary or available during the discussion period.

There are some who differ with me, but I believe that most recommendations, if not all, should be approved by the board if the manager recommends them. If a manager brings a large number of recommendations to the board which are turned down, the organization probably needs a new manager. As a director, I want recommendations to be brought to me which are thoroughly researched, carefully analyzed, and can be approved with comfort and conviction.

Directors should raise questions and express reservations, if there are any. Directors may even try to talk the manager out of an idea, but if he persists, I am inclined to allow him to try his plan, unless it carries the risk of seriously damaging or destroying the cooperative. Even though the board is ultimately charged with managing the affairs of the cooperative, they must delegate the responsibility and authority to a full time professional manager. My philosophy is to employ a manager, give him advice, and counsel but let him manage, judge his performance, and replace him if the results are not satisfactory.

We have tried to demonstrate that board policy includes purpose, action goals and objectives. A summary of the board policy process is shown in exhibit 39.

```
┌─────────────────────────────────────────────────────────┐
│                  Board Policy Process                     │
│                  ────────────────────                     │
│                                                           │
│   Consideration of Policy Options          Board-Staff    │
│   Policy Determination                           Board    │
│   Policy Implementation              Board and/or Staff    │
│   Policy Monitoring                         Board-Staff    │
│                                                           │
└─────────────────────────────────────────────────────────┘

┌─────────────────────────────────────────────────────────┐
│          Policy Implementation — Staff                    │
│          ─────────────────────────────                    │
│              Staff Management Through                     │
│             Administrative Procedures                     │
│                Based on Board Policy                      │
└─────────────────────────────────────────────────────────┘
```

Exhibit 39

Three of the four steps are achieved by board/staff together. Only in policy determination does the board act alone. Note particularly that at the third step, implementation, both board and staff implement. This means that the board must accept responsibility for the results of selected policies. This will be discussed in chapter 7. We have heard many times that "the board decides, staff do." This is not true.

Exhibit 40 describes the most and the least that boards implement. The most, of course, is a pure voluntary organization. The least is a fully staffed voluntary organization.

Each of these will be discussed in chapter 8 with the exception of investments.

If an organization has an endowment, the management of that endowment is the *job* responsibility of the board of directors. The responsibility for investment should never be delegated to staff.

In chapter 3, we stated that the board of directors is responsible for *all* that happens within its organization. Read this statement carefully:

Boards may delegate, they may not abdicate.

The Board and Policy Implementation

		At Most	At Least	
Policies	Management			• Policy Determination • Sanction/Linkage • Staff Relationships
	Program Services			• Advocacy
	Business			• Investments
	Personnel			• Staff Chief Executive Retention Performance Appraisal • Image
	Resource Development			• Volunteers • Support

©IVO

Board → [|] ← Staff

Exhibit 40

Boards are responsible for what they delegate. The board may delegate a policy to the executive. The executive in turn delegates to the assistant executive director. The assistant executive director delegates to the program supervisor. The program supervisor delegates to the social worker.

The board of directors is responsible for what the social worker does. It has delegated the authority to the executive director to hire the social worker and holds the executive responsible for what the social worker does. Exhibit 41 is a definition of authority, responsibility, and accountability.

With this in mind, it is *most important to note* that the board does not simply determine policy. Determination has three parts:

1. Policy determination—the decision to do it.

2. Who is held accountable for the results of the policy.

3. The authority to carry it out.

Many boards stop at the first point, which gives way to frustra-

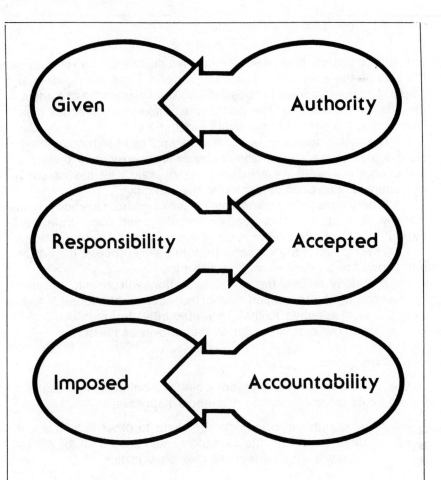

Authority — is the right to use discretion in developing the targets necessary to assume the achievement of established objectives.

Responsibility — is the obligation of a subordinate to perform duties which have been assigned and accepted.

Accountability — is answerable not only for end results but for the actions that bring about the end results.

IVO

Exhibit 41

tion and confusion. Boards sometimes decide they will do something, then blame the executive if it doesn't happen. Fund raising is an example. The board agrees to raise $100,000 and blames the executive if the goal is not reached. The board must make accountability clear. Remember, the board cannot avoid number 2.

Number 3, authority, is also a problem. The board makes a decision, delegates the accountability clearly to the executive, then hires the executive's staff! As Mr. Sims clearly said, "let the executive manage what has been delegated to the executive."

Where does policy come from? It can come from anybody. Realistically, 90% of the policy recommendations will come from staff. Exhibit 42 is a graphic description of the policy formulation process.

The top half represents the smooth policy process; the bottom half shows the process when it is disrupted.

Hopefully, most of the recommendations will come to the board from a committee. Once again most of the recommendations will come from the staff assigned to the committee after thorough discussion with all staff. The recommendation then moves as illustrated.

Two points:

1. The committee is responsible for monitoring the results of its recommendation if the board approves.

2. Although the board can delegate to other than the staff chief executive, the executive must keep track of all that happens which affects his/her organization.

Concerning the lower half of exhibit 42, the board of directors must have some mechanism to allow clients and the community to contribute their expertise into its deliberations. Board volunteers have direct access; interested others do not.

Suppose an issue of a policy nature comes to the board of which the staff has neither seen nor heard. What happens? Our view is that board meetings are not staff meetings and staff have no role except when asked to respond to something. This will be discussed in chapter 11. However, if the board does decide to discuss and decide the issue, the staff has the right to offer input, even to the extent of requesting the issue be tabled until staff has reviewed it.

If the board refers to a committee, then the staff input goes through the committee. When the issue returns to the board, staff has no further input.

The bottom line to the board for administration is the grievance

Policy Formulation

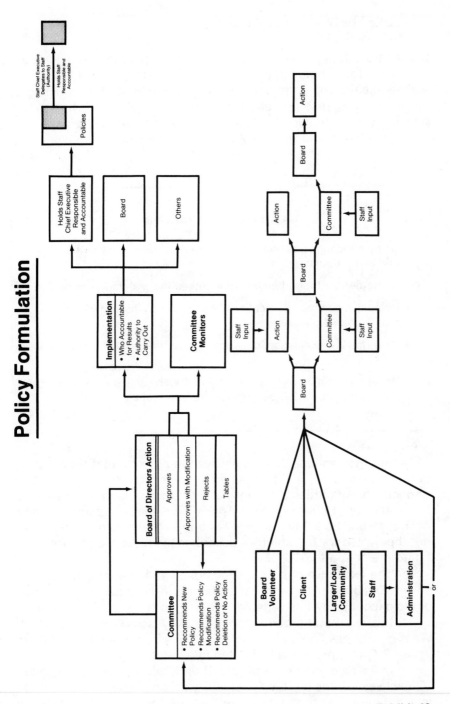

Exhibit 42

procedure. It is important that the board make clear with what the staff may come to the board. If the board allows too much staff input about management it will undercut the ability of the executive to manage.

The grievance procedure should confine itself to issues in the personnel management division only and should be exclusive of performance. Exhibit 43 shows examples of grievances.

SAMPLE OF GRIEVANCES

—Being hired for a position and given a salary that is outside the range and level stipulated in the personnel policies.

—Being denied fringe benefits guaranteed in the personnel policies.

—Being denied time off (vacations, absence, etc.) that is guaranteed in the personnel policies.

—Performance evaluation conducted in violation of the personnel policies.

—Being hired for a position and finding that the actual work does not correspond to the job description presented at the interview.

Exhibit 43

In organizations there is always the problem of distinguishing between democracy and discipline. The democracy is up to the point of decision. All parties are involved in the discussion and, in specific cases, the vote. However, once a decision is made, discipline must take over. Staff and board members are bound by the decision—whether or not they voted for it. Exhibit 44 describes the response of a staff or a board member after a decision.

The executive *does* influence policy and affect the balance of power. Exhibit 45 shows some of the factors in the increasing influence of the executive by this variable increase.

In a multi-unit organization, the policy issue is quite important. What constitutes "policy" at the unit level as opposed to "corporate policy"? Our approach is illustrated in exhibit 46.

In a single unit organization, "Board Policy" continues through "Objectives." In the multi-unit voluntary organization, however, there is a difference: The board of directors, or corporate policy, carries

---

Organizational Democracy and Discipline

Staff/Board Member Response after Decision

1. Total Implementation

2. Total Implementation, Work
   for Change

3. Resign

Exhibit 44

---

through "Action Goals"; then the board of managers, or unit boards, make the decisions concerning objectives, but always within the board of directors or corporate policy.

However, a certain degree of flexibility exists in each of the management divisions. The greatest is a program services. A unit can offer whatever programs it wishes as long as they fit within corporate action goals. (Recall chapter 4—Hierarchy of Planning.) A unit will have to recommend to the corporate board of directors that corporate action goals be changed if some of their programs remain outside corporate action goals.

However, *all* units must report statistics, as an example, in the same way. In business there is little flexibility. A multi-unit cannot have its units budgeting in different ways. Budget formats are the same. What the budget contains is unit policy. In personnel, salaries, job descriptions, who is hired, and at what level are unit decisions. Exhibit 47 illustrates this flexibility.

Before closing this chapter, the issues of power and manipulation require examination. *The Random House Dictionary of the English Language* (Unabridged Edition) contains the following primary definition of *manipulate*: "to handle, manage, or use, especially with skill, in some process of treatment or performance." Unfortunately, the other definitions of manipulate employ these synonyms: "to juggle, falsify."

Executive Influence

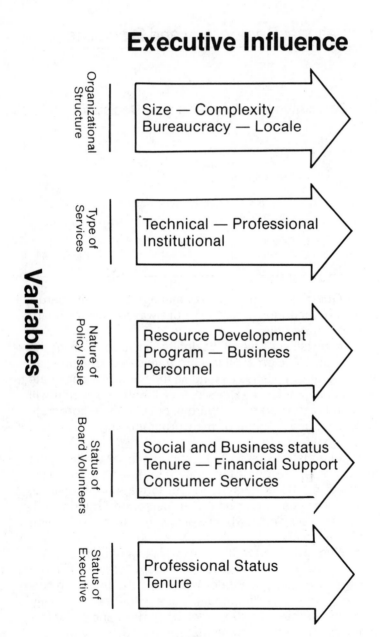

Variables

Organizational Structure	Size — Complexity Bureaucracy — Locale
Type of Services	Technical — Professional Institutional
Nature of Policy Issue	Resource Development Program — Business Personnel
Status of Board Volunteers	Social and Business status Tenure — Financial Support Consumer Services
Status of Executive	Professional Status Tenure

Balance of Power and Policy Influence

Exhibit 45

Definition of Policy for a Multi-Unit Organization

Single-Unit Organization:	Multi-Unit Organization:
Board Policy	Board of Directors or Corporate Policy
Board Policy	Board of Managers Or Unit Policy Within Corporate Policy of Purpose. Purpose Goals. Action Goals
Staff Implementation	Staff Implementation

Purpose				
Purpose Goals	Purpose Goals	Purpose Goals	Purpose Goals	Purpose Goals

Action Goals	Action Goals	Action Goals	Action Goals	Action Goals

Objective	Objective	Objective

Target	Target	Target

Exhibit 46

Unit Policy Flexibility in Multi-Unit Organization

Personnel	Business	Resource Development	Program Services	Management

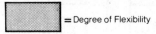 = Degree of Flexibility

Exhibit 47

The point is that staff has the responsibility to assist its board volunteers in succeeding in the pursuit of the lawful purpose, goals, and objectives of their organization. This is not manipulation in its darkest sense; it is positive motivation. Where manipulation takes on a negative connotation is in the exercise of the staff's power. Staff, especially in education, has been concerned with power—or, rather, its lack of it. It contends that, if boards have the power to set and dictate policy, then it—the staff—is essentially powerless to influence the decision-making process. What it generally overlooks is that it has the greater, more subtle power; the *power of persuasion.*

Part of this power of persuasion is a product of the power of knowledge. By virtue of his being full time, the staff executive has more knowledge about the operational aspects of the particular organization and its requirements than has the board volunteer. Dr. H. Durward Hofler deals with this issue very well in his paper, "Voluntary Organizations":

> Knowledge is a form of power and control; by implication, lack of knowledge means a loss of power and control. Thus, for example, withhold-

ing and/or providing misleading information is not an uncommon means of controlling another person's behavior against what would be his will were he given fuller, more accurate information.

Further on, Dr. Hofler contends:

> . . . real decision-making power often is in the hands of information processors instead of in the hands of those who formally make decisions.[1]

In this context, the information processor is the staff member; the decision-maker, the board member. This can be illustrated as in exhibit 48.

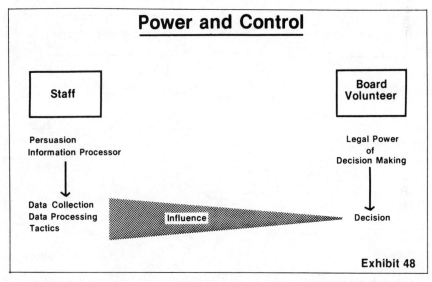

Power and Control

Staff

Board Volunteer

Persuasion
Information Processor

Legal Power
of
Decision Making

Data Collection
Data Processing
Tactics

Influence

Decision

Exhibit 48

While this process is natural and can be advantageous when there is trust, as the staff begins to withhold or process information or data to influence decisions of board volunteers, it becomes truly manipulative in the sinister sense. There is no quicker way for the trust between board volunteer and staff to be destroyed than through the "processing" of information by the staff in order to influence board decisions. It sets a terrible trap into which it is easy to fall and must be continuously guarded against.

> When I entered "into service" here, I determined that, happen what would, I *never* would intrigue among the committee. Now I perceive that I do all my business by intrigue. I propose in private, to A, B, or C

the resolution I think A, B, or C most capable of carrying in committee, and then leave it to them, and I always win.

Florence Nightingale

In modern terminology, this is called "getting your ducks in order." What is destructive, as stated, is "processing." Exhibit 49 illustrates this.

Manipulation

Staff		Board Volunteers		
Facts		Mr. Smith	Mr. Brown	Mr. Jones
A		Facts	Facts	Facts
B		A	B	A
C		B	C	B
D		C	D	C
E		F	E	D
F				F

Exhibit 49

Staff has facts A through F. It is selective in who gets the facts to influence a decision. It may work once, even twice; but once it is found out, trust evaporates.

Policy can be defined in many different ways. To avoid the ambiguity of language we again suggest that "policy must be *seen* to be defined." This requires a basic management concept as described in chapter 4. Without this, confusion will always arise such as: What is policy? and What is implementation?

NOTES

1. H. Durward Hofler, "Voluntary Organizations" (Unpublished paper, Evanston, Illinois: Systems Facilitation Association, Inc., 1971).

THE FUNCTION OF THE BOARD OF DIRECTORS AND THE ROLE OF THE BOARD VOLUNTEER

8

Some people answer the question "What do boards of directors do?" with a long list of activities. Others make a long list of jobs for board volunteers. Rarely does anyone differentiate between the functions of the two entities.

In actuality, these long lists seem to list the *behavioral requirements for role and outcomes* of what they do, rather than actual functions. Functions, role, behavior, and outcomes must be separated. This chapter will not attempt to separate all the possibilities. Instead, only the function, role, and behavior will be defined—leaving outcomes to the reader to identify. Examples of these include:

Policy Decision—board of directors—*Function*

Discussion and one vote—board volunteers—*Role*

Attend board and committee meetings—*Behavior requirement*

Continuity—*Outcome*

Function of the Board

The board is a group with certain functions. These functions are the result of the role its group members (board volunteers) play. The function of the board as a group or whole is shown in exhibit 50.

In a representative democratic form of government, this is known as the legislative branch. A board does *four* things. The preceding chapters have described in detail what each of the four functions mean.

Governing Board Function

Establishes Planning Framework within which the Board:

Determines policy (effectiveness)

Implements selected policies

Monitors policy implementation (efficiency)

Legislative — Advice and Consent

Exhibit 50

Role of the Volunteer

Now to the board volunteers. What roles do they fill as individuals? Exhibit 51 is a summary of the five roles of a board volunteer. Although long lists of roles can be made, these five roles have been designed to incorporate all of them.

In examining each of the five roles, remember that the specific action taken by the board volunteers comes from the planning of the programming at the object and target levels.

Role 1—Policy

Each board volunteer has one vote in the determination of policy. Actually, there may be *two* votes—one at the committee level to make a policy recommendation to the board and one at the board level to make the recommendation a policy.

A board volunteer could vote with the minority at the committee level, but find his vote at the board level in the majority—or the reverse.

Role 2—Resource Development

Every board volunteer has a role to play in the area of resource development; but resource development is more than just raising money. True, board volunteers have the responsibility to provide funds to implement the policy decisions they make. Yet this is only one of a triad of resources for a voluntary organization, as illustrated in exhibit 52.

Role of the Board Volunteer

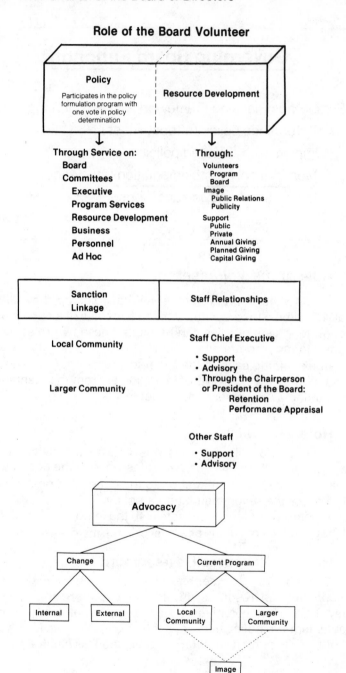

Policy
Participates in the policy
formulation program with
one vote in policy
determination

Resource Development

Through Service on:
Board
Committees
    Executive
    Program Services
    Resource Development
    Business
    Personnel
    Ad Hoc

Through:
Volunteers
  Program
  Board
Image
  Public Relations
  Publicity
Support
  Public
  Private
  Annual Giving
  Planned Giving
  Capital Giving

Sanction
Linkage

Staff Relationships

Local Community

Larger Community

Staff Chief Executive

- **Support**
- **Advisory**
- **Through the Chairperson**
  or President of the Board:
      Retention
      Performance Appraisal

Other Staff

- **Support**
- **Advisory**

Advocacy

Change

Current Program

Internal

External

Local
Community

Larger
Community

Image

Exhibit 51

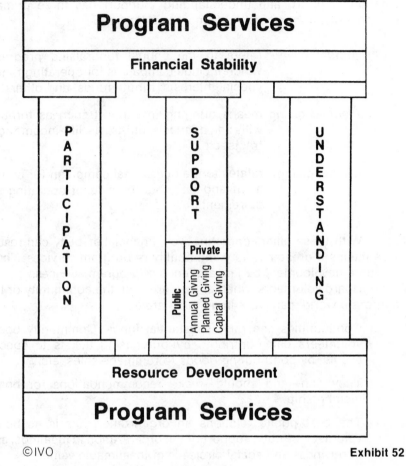

©IVO

Exhibit 52

Support—public and private dollars

Participation (Volunteers)—people involved and committed

Understanding (Image)—enhancing the public image

Board volunteers have the responsibility to function in all three areas. Program services are the foundation upon which resource development is built. People will not become involved, money cannot be raised, and a positive public image will not be generated unless the services offered to clients merit that result.

As stated earlier, resource development has three pillars: participation, support, and understanding. Support has three primary components: *annual, planned*, and *capital giving.*

Annual giving refers to the annual fundraising programs which include campaigns for operating funds, special interests, tribute funds, and others.

Planned giving means bringing in support such as through wills and bequests, uni-trusts, life-income contracts, etc.

Capital giving relates to the occasional campaign for equipment and buildings outside of operating requirements.

With these pillars operating well, financial stability can result. This means a greater variety and quality of program services. Thus, resource development begins and ends in program services.

Board volunteers, whether they are from the community or the corporate world, can work in all three areas:

Communities can raise substantial funds. Community board volunteers can contribute by purchasing tickets to special events, by contributing goods to rummage sales, etc.

They can—and should—make recommendations for board membership.

The best public relations an organization has is its board volunteers. Public support of the organization in meetings, and in business and social circles is of inestimable value.

In addition, community board volunteers can also support organizations through the contribution of time in program services.

Board volunteers may serve on several different committees, but they *all* have responsibility toward resource development.

Role 3—Sanction/Linkage

Sanction: Board volunteers give us the right to exist as an organization. They legitimize the organization. "Local Community" refers to the immediate locale of the organization, where those served by the organization reside. "Larger Community" refers to those community segments outside the local community. In urban areas there is a considerable difference between the two. In rural and suburban areas, this distinction is less clearly defined.

In our urban areas, organizations formerly needed the sanction of the larger communities in order to exist, as the fund money for organizations came from there. Little attention was given to the wishes or issues of the local communities. The revolution of the sixties changed all this. Local communities demanded participation in the decision-making process of the institutions located in their communities. The implications for voluntary organizations were—and are—staggering. Basically, it meant that an urban-area organization could be put out of business by the withdrawal of support from *two* communities: the larger community could withdraw the cash; the local community could withdraw the constituency. Either withdrawal spelled certain extinction for any affected organization. Bona fide sanction is required from both sectors.

Linkage: The best interpreters or links to the communities in which organizations operate are the board volunteers. Informed, committed volunteers know their respective communities and the constituencies within them. They know how to approach people for donations of money, time, space, services or any other items needed by organizations.

Role 4—Staff Relationships

There are two relationships: one with the staff chief executive and the other with other staff. The relationship between a staff chief executive and his staff is crucial to the operational effectiveness of an organization. This is a difficult, ongoing task and one which, unfortunately, is sometimes touched upon lightly, if at all. A helpful Voluntary Management Press publication is: *The Performance Appraisal of the Staff Chief Executive.*

The relationship between the staff executive and his/her board volunteers—collectively and individually—provides the environment within which a voluntary organization functions. If members within this relationship have the basic ingredients of trust, candor, and respect, and both the ability and desire to resolve conflicts, the organization will function smoothly. Should those ingredients be missing, conflict and immobilization will prevail.

Acquiring.   Hiring of the staff chief executive is one of the board's most crucial policy decisions. As broad a spectrum of board-volunteer participation as possible is important in this action. A screening or search committee may be appointed to identify a new executive. However, the board should set up guidelines such as the following for the committee:

1. Comprehensive criteria for the selection of candidates.

2. Comprehensive job description to be filled.

3. Tentative time frame for locating candidates for the position. A hasty or casual recruitment decision can set the organization back.

4. Actual appointment of the screening or search committee. This might include preliminary interviewing to reach two or three candidates for the board interview.

5. Maintenance of candor during the entire process. Should either side gloss over or obscure distasteful facts, distrust may readily arise and jeopardize any existing meaningful relationship.

Support.   When a board retains a staff chief executive, it accepts an obligation to support that executive. Too many boards retain a chief executive, then abandon him when controversy arises. If a board cannot support its chief executive, either the membership on the board must be changed or a new executive must be hired.

In the final analysis, the staff chief executive's strength vis-à-vis his staff, community and clients depends upon the support of the board. Constant conflict between the board and its chief executive will undermine the entire organization.

Supervision.   The staff chief executive is under the supervision of the board. Every book ever written about boards stresses this fact. There is nothing wrong with this—unless each member of the board attempts to "supervise" the executive. The key point here is that all matters pertaining to the chief executive should go through the chairperson of the board. Too frequently, a staff is immobilized by a flood of requests or directions from individual board members. This is not to say that the committee chairperson cannot make requests of the key staff person related to his committee. It simply means that, to insure good communications and to avoid conflicting or confusing requests:

1. General organizational requests of the staff chief executive should go through the board chairperson.

2. Requests of the staff from committee members should go through the committee chairperson.

Performance Appraisal.   Unfortunately, staff-executive performance appraisal generally ensues only at points of crisis, rather than from a systematic process. This task is frequently left in the hands of the board chairperson. A staff executive can always help by requesting that periodic appraisals be made or a definite procedure be established.

The process of appraisal should be delegated to the personnel committee under the direction of the chairperson of the board. The final appraisal should be the decision of the board of directors. The single most important policy decision that the board makes is the performance appraisal of the staff chief executive.

Advice.   Board volunteers should be free to offer advice to the executive. Likewise, the executive should be able to seek advice from the board or individual board volunteers. An open, collaborative relationship is essential for organizational growth and development.

Individual board volunteers must remember that they have no power to "tell" the executive what to do. The power to "direct" the executive rests only with the total board. In sum:

Policy formulation   —Board volunteers and staff advise board together.

Policy determination   —Board alone.

Policy implementation—If delegated to the executive, then the board becomes a group of advisors.

Role 5—Advocacy

There are two kinds of advocacy:

Current program—helping to create a positive organizational image. The current program aspect of image has been discussed.

Change   —which is resorting to higher authority, either internally or externally, to request that something be changed or not changed.

Internal: Each board volunteer has an internal advocacy role. In policy discussions a board volunteer advocates his/her viewpoint. A committee chairperson advocates the committee's position.

External: Going to external authority whose decisions could affect an organization. Each board volunteer should participate in at least one of these activities:

1. Appear as a spokesperson or speaker.
2. Appear as a group member.
3. Write.

Exhibit 53 gives some guidelines for "Behavior."

GUIDELINES FOR SUCCESSFUL BOARD VOLUNTEER STEWARDSHIP

Regularly, attend board and committee meetings.

Read and understand the minutes of board meetings and the minutes of your committee assignments.

Read your organization's publications.

Treat the affairs of your organization as you would your own.

Be certain your organization's records are audited by a reputable CPA firm.

Understand your organization's goals, objectives, and programs; how they are decided and implemented.

Insist that all committee meetings be reported at board meetings in either oral or written form.

Know your organization's budget, budgeting process, and financial situation.

Know who is authorized to sign checks and to what amount.

Avoid self-serving policies.

Inquire if there is something you do not understand, or if something comes to your attention which causes you to question a policy or practice.

Insist that there be a well-established personnel program with a competent staff chief executive.

Exhibit 53(a)

We are often asked about the optimum size of a board of directors. We offer a gauge: 15–17 to 35–40. If a board gets below 15 to 17 members, there is a real danger of becoming "incestful." "Group think" takes over. If a board gets beyond 40, decision-making slows down, giving rise to the dangers of control by executive committee. Use of non-board members on committees can increase the involvement of significant others without increasing the board.

The final role a board volunteer can play is as a program volun-

---

Avoid the substance or appearance of conflict of interest, either fiscal or programatic.

Be certain your organization is fulfilling all aspects of its not-for-profit and tax exempt status.

Insist on a written procedure for board membership and nominating committee procedure.

Monitor the community and professional image of your organization.

Be certain that "policies" are clearly identified and that the board acts on them as a group rather than as a small group of individuals.

Know your organization's board of directors, programs, and staff before you accept membership.

Require that your organization have proper legal counsel, not a board volunteer.

Monitor the activity of your executive committee to insure it does not overstep its authority.

Insist that the board have a policy relative to board volunteer liability.

Follow through with dispatch on your organization's commitments.

Understand the difference between staff and board functions, staff and board roles, and policy and implementation.

Recognize that staff members have other responsibilities apart from work with the board. Do not ask for information requiring extensive research without first consulting with the chairperson or the board.

Exhibit 53(b)

teer. Many times a board member volunteers to deliver or assist in the delivery of a policy that has been delegated to staff. This presents a problem both to the board volunteer and to staff. Board volunteers must be aware of their role changes. A staff must work with the board volunteer as it would with any other volunteer.

The following statement sums up the role of the board volunteer well: "Board volunteers must place the larger interests of the organization above personal or factional concerns."

THE FUNCTION OF STAFF AND THE ROLES OF STAFF MEMBERS

9

As with the board of directors, a distinction must be made between the function of the staff, as a group, and the role of the individual staff member. Staff functions are listed in exhibit 54.

Staff Function

Participates in and supports the Board Policy Process

Supports the Board in the Board's implementation of selected policies

Administers the implementation of Board policies which have been delegated to the staff and for which $\frac{\text{the Board}}{\text{Executive}}$ holds the Staff Chief Executive accountable.

Exhibit 54

In the board policy process, such duties as data collection, meetings, announcements, and duplication are the staff's job in supporting the policy process.

Supporting the board presents a problem. At times a board tends to require so much time for its function that staff work begins to suffer. A board must guard against "capturing" a staff, then castigating it for not completing work effectively and efficiently.

The third function has been discussed in previous chapters.

If we envision the voluntary organization as resting on top of an arch in a wall, the board volunteers are represented by the bricks in the wall and staff by the arch. The blocks in the arch are representative of a variety of names used to describe staff; there are many others. The point here is that the keystone—that which holds the entire organization together—is the staff executive's role as an enabler vis-à-vis his board volunteers.

Role of the Staff Member

Voluntary Organization

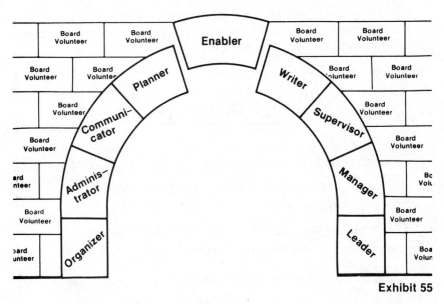

Exhibit 55

The term *enabler* is subject to many interpretations. Exhibit 56 shows what "enabler" means in the context of a voluntary organization.

In this context, the staff supports board volunteers by:

1. *Providing a cause in which to believe.* To be effective, every board volunteer must be proud of the voluntary organization he serves. He must be able to identify with the purpose of the

- A CAUSE TO BELIEVE IN
- A FRAMEWORK WITHIN WHICH TO WORK
- SPECIFIC TASKS TO BE ACCOMPLISHED
- DEADLINES FOR TASKS TO BE ACCOMPLISHED
- AN OPPORTUNITY TO PARTICIPATE IN THE
  DECISIONS THAT AFFECT THE FIRST FOUR

SUPPORTED BY
PROMPT, ACCURATE AND SUSTAINED ASSISTANCE

Exhibit 56

organization—to represent it, where necessary, with confidence and conviction.

2. *Providing a framework within which to work.* During the recruitment process, a board volunteer usually asks: "Where do I fit?" In other words: "What is the framework within which I must work?" He wants to know precisely his place in the realm of the organizational structure and operations.

3. *Providing specific tasks to be accomplished.* The next question asked is: "What do you want me to do?" It is important that staff provide those tasks which need to be accomplished.

4. *Providing deadlines for tasks to be accomplished.* The question which follows is: "When do you want this done?" Staff must have a definite calendar in mind for the tasks which are to be accomplished by board volunteers.

5. *Providing an opportunity to participate in the decisions that affect the first four points.* This is the key. In the first four points, the implication is made that staff literally "provides" all these items for board volunteers. If, in fact, this happens,

a board or committee will merely follow the lead of the staff, giving only superficial attention to the issues of the organization. Hence, it is most important that board volunteers have an opportunity to discuss and decide those issues raised by the first four items.

A board volunteer made an interesting statement to us. He said: "Don't ask me what I think—ask me what I think about what *you* think, then we'll get something done."

The message is clear—do your homework. Come to me with data and your conclusions. I'll add mine and we'll get the job done. I don't have the time to formulate all the data and options. Board volunteers take initiative from staff initiative. They are only as effective as staff wishes or helps them to be; rarely do they take over and actually "lead" the voluntary organization.

Another board volunteer once said, "God help us if the board decides to take the initiative all the time."

All these items must be supported by prompt, accurate, and sustained assistance on the part of the staff. The subject of "professionalism" is a much-debated topic within voluntary organizations, usually centering around one point: the mastery of a prescribed body of knowledge leading to a set of professional degrees. Degrees are fine and necessary, but to board volunteers they are of secondary importance. Board volunteers are successful only to the extent that they are supported by their staff. Let a staff member fail to return a phone call, provide inaccurate or late information, or embarrass a board volunteer and all the knowledge and degrees in the world will not support him. Board volunteers expect from their staff competence and personal integrity. They expect performance to keep pace with promises. They expect satisfaction with both direction and pace. Staff must remember, too, that board volunteers expect reasoned responses, not "I think." Most of all, board volunteers should be able to predict the behavior of their staff. Consistency is the key.

Exhibit 57 lists some guidelines for staff.

STAFF GUIDELINES FOR SUCCESSFUL BOARD RELATIONSHIPS

1. Recognize that board volunteers are vital to staff and organizational success.

2. Believe that board volunteers join to assist, not to take over.

3. Be dependable, accurate, and prompt in the relationship.

4. Do not expect board volunteers to take initiative in a vacuum; do your homework.

5. Make working with the board of directors an integral part of the job description, rather than an "add on."

6. Do not use a board relationship to air organizational complaints.

7. Understand the difference between staff and board function, staff and board roles, and policy and implementation.

8. Coordinate and accurately provide sufficient data; but do not adapt it to achieve personal ends.

Exhibit 57

THE DELICATE BALANCE

10

A voluntary organization is delicately balanced. Graphically, it looks like exhibit 58.

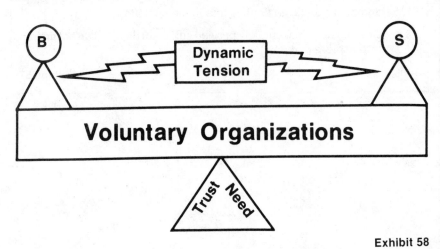

Exhibit 58

It balances when board volunteers and staff each understand and accept their respective roles. There is a tension between the two. For the staff member, it is based on the realization that the more he/she involves board volunteers, the greater his/her accountability. For the board volunteer, it is in the realization that when in committing to board membership, his/her reputation becomes, to a large degree, dependent on staff. This tension need not be debilitating; it should be dynamic and creative. It is healthy and constructive. This is a push-pull effect.

The main supports of the relationship are trust and need. Staff must understand that board volunteers join to help, not to interfere in operations or to take over. The objective is better understanding because understanding breeds confidence—and confidence leads to trust. Without trust we have nothing. Board and staff need each other. In the last analysis, neither can succeed without the other.

Exhibit 59 illustrates one way a voluntary organization can go out of balance: when it is overly staff-oriented.

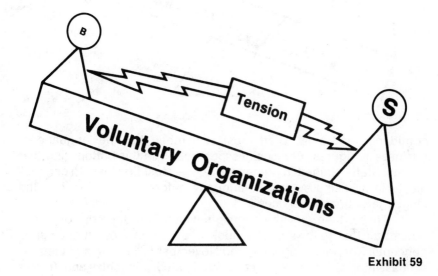

Exhibit 59

Here, board volunteers are reduced to "yea-sayers." Generally, when confronted with this situation, the good board volunteers depart rather quickly! Voluntarism is in trouble today partly because this has happened to so many of our voluntary organizations. It is interesting to note that the financial troubles of voluntary organizations are not really *financial*, but *board* problems. Uninvolved board volunteers will not fund an organization. Those organizations in financial trouble are out of balance because of over-professionalism. Trust and need have vanished. Dynamic tension has slackened and become simple *tension*.

Exhibit 60 represents another way a voluntary organization falls out of balance. It becomes overly board-oriented without staff involvement. As in exhibit 59, trust and need vanish. Dynamic tension again simply becomes *tension*.

Communication between board and staff is what holds it all together. Communication leads to understanding from which can flow

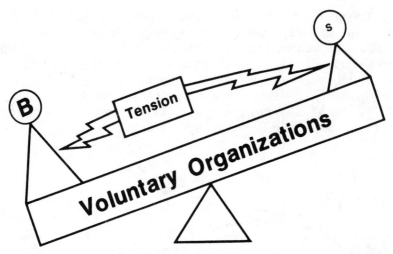

Exhibit 60

confidence and trust. Staff must remember that the language of business is figures. For businesspersons, it is the bottom line that counts. Staff—trained in human services—must first learn to communicate in a businessperson's language before it can move into the language of human services.

These, then, are the concepts which form the core of voluntarism; all that follows in this book is based on these fundamental concepts. The following appeared November 5, 1973, in a column by Ambassador Charles W. Yost, a syndicated columnist and former United States diplomat. It says much about the current malaise of voluntary organizations:

> The practitioners of every profession have a congenital tendency to believe that they are wiser than the layman, that he lacks the training and insight on which sound judgments must be based and that he should therefore not be confused by awkward facts that might upset him.
>
> This line of argument is, of course, a rationalization. What the expert really means is that, by virtue of his superior understanding and exclusive sources of information, he knows best, not only for himself but for everyone else; and that he does not want the ill-informed to complain, criticize, perhaps even upset the applecart he has with great pains put on the road.[1]

There was a time when our voluntary organizations were *totally* volunteer. An organization was created to meet a need, and all its functions were performed by volunteers: funding, program, budget, janitorial work, and so forth. As these organizations grew more complex, volunteers hired the first "professional" staff to handle the day-to-day operations of the organization.

Over a period of years, many voluntary organizations lost "the delicate balance" between board volunteer and staff. A convenient *modus operandi* began to emerge. Boards of directors began to limit their board meetings to social gatherings where they gave sanction to the decisions of the staff. Boards followed the "wisdom" of their hand-picked chief executive, withholding their own wisdom.

United Funds tended to support this drift toward over-professionalism. As the funding of voluntary organizations became more centrally managed, the boards of directors had less and less responsibility to raise funds *directly* for their organizations. Their funding efforts were directed toward a central source (United Fund). Then they went to that source, as members of a board of directors, to request a portion of the source for their own organization. This was, in effect, raising money twice: once, for the central source directly; then, to the source for their own organizations. This was a process of indirect fund raising.

This procedure led board members to feel that they were asking the central source for some of *its* money, and thus policy decisions on expenditures were based upon spending "somebody else's money," all of which tended to weaken a board's desire to participate very deeply in those decisions. After all, they could always ask "them" for more money. The point is that the more involved members of a board are in funding, the more attention they will pay to how the money is spent, because *they* have raised it.

The trend toward over-professionalism reached its high point in the late affluent sixties. The condition was—and is—well described by Charles A. Nelson, a principal in the New York office of Peat, Marwick, Mitchell and Co.:

> In serene contrast to the restlessness of the current scene, does the lay board of trustees of a college, a hospital or a charitable organization represent the old stability, respect for the old order, a rare refuge of sensibility and tradition? I am afraid not—not for long anyway—for the lay board of trustees as an institution is under attack. While for some it may be viewed as the Establishment personified, of perhaps greater importance are characterizations that are often made by those genuinely interested in furthering the progress of the institution.
>
> Our governing boards, it is said, are made up of people who are too old, who tolerate conflicts of interest, who do not know enough about

the institutions to govern them, who tend to be chosen from a narrow sector of the public and not to be sensitive to broad public interests. They tend to stay in office too long, it is said; they do not appreciate the need for turnover, and they do not give enough time to their jobs.

Mr. Nelson states:

The notion of minimal involvement cannot withstand critical inspection; it can lead—it has led—to most profound errors in the governance of our institutions. The board will not be competent to hire the right man for chief executive if its role is limited to that function. It cannot possibly know enough about what the needs of that institution are, the nature of the problems that man will have to face, to be able to provide the right description of the man who might fill that post.

In order to know whom to hire, the board must know where the institution is and where it should be going. Unless the trustees are exceedingly well informed about the nature of the institution and its needs, understand its present problems, and have a profound conviction about the nature of the enterprises going on there, their judgment as to what that institution needs will undoubtedly be faulty. They can easily make the wrong choice.

Furthermore, the argument for the minimal trustee role hides a curiously unreal assessment of the chief executive. Is he in fact typically infallible in his judgments? Even the superior man—Is he not in in need of consultation with a balanced and objective body? I regret to say that I can name all too large a number of private institutions which are in deep trouble today because, under the leadership of "strong" presidents in the '50's and '60's, they made mistaken judgments about the future of their institutions, incurring substantial debt in the process, and in the absence of the corrective judgments which an active, well-informed board of trustees should have supplied.[2]

The reasons for the abrupt halt in the trend toward professionalizing our voluntary organizations, and for their increasing troubles, are many and varied. It may be useful to cite a few.

1. Communities, especially urban ones, are demanding a greater voice in the decisions that result in program services which are supposed to benefit them.

2. Staff alignments are changing; minorities are assuming more and more positions of authority in their organizations.

3. Communities are no longer satisfied with symptom treatment. If rats are biting the feet of sleeping children, com-

munities will not accept a gift of a thousand rat-traps; they want the *cause* of the rats eradicated.

4. United Fund drives are "topping off." United Ways and Community Funds are becoming much more influential, even though their ability to raise increasing amounts of money is topping off. The groups are adopting "program priorities" to facilitate the distribution of available dollars. Member organizations are increasingly under pressure to conform to priorities or face the loss of allocations.

5. Contributors are becoming more selective, preferring to give to specific programs rather than to organizations.

6. More and more, corporations are accepting the premise of corporate responsibility to society and its problems.

7. Boards and staffs are being forced to become more representative of the communities they serve.

8. Social and technological change is escalating at a pace undreamed of five years ago.

9. There is a greater emphasis on, and pride in, one's cultural heritage.

10. Staff autocracy is weakening as board volunteers are increasingly demanding a role in management, unwilling to follow blindly the staff leadership.

11. There is a proliferation of voluntary organizations, and their dollar requirements are escalating much faster than the contributors' ability or desire to give.

12. Similar and dissimilar organizations are required to collaborate, especially in urban areas.

13. The Equal Rights movement requires organizations to be cognizant of racial, ethnic, and sex balance.

All these factors have brought about a dramatic change in the management of voluntary organizatons. They can no longer run quietly along with their staff making decisions and their boards "yea-saying." The roles of the staff and the board volunteers must be redefined, the delicate balance restored.

The authors have seen many voluntary organizations that claim to be "in trouble" usually because they can't raise money. The malaise almost invariably turns out to be the deterioration of the board-volunteer/staff relationship. Such conditions have put tremendous pressure on staff to bring their organizations back into balance; in reality, they are quite unprepared to do this. Complacency has spawned bad habits and loss of understanding of the true purposes of the voluntary organization.

The present status of the staff executive was well described by Dr. Thomas R. Bennett II, during an address to the 1966 graduating class of George Williams College:

> I hope you can bring about the kind of society which accepts the inevitability of the conflict between person and culture; between person and organization; but is willing to try to find rational grounds for the mediation of the conflict.[3]

All these pressures have resulted in an enormous escalation in the degree of accountability of the staff executive to his board and community. He is no longer in the position of having his decisions rubber-stamped. More and more, he is being held accountable for his decisions and thus needs more data and board sanction to undergird those decisions. With every increase in involvement of board volunteers in the decision making process of the organization, there follows an equal—or greater—increase in staff accountability.

The situation is an extremely tense one. Both staff and board volunteers seek the dynamic, creative balance between professional dominance (which results in rubber-stamp boards) and lay dominance (which results in arrogation of the operational authority of the staff and eventual loss of purpose). They are unaccustomed to this new arrangement; thus, the process of developing it must be carefully nurtured.

There is a simple truth in the present climate of voluntary organizations: the staff executive dramatically increases his success potential if he has a harmonious, trustful, and respectful relationship with his board of directors. This does not mean the elimination of conflict, but its successful management. An otherwise competent staff chief executive may well be dismissed because he/she is unable to find and maintain "the delicate balance" with the board of directors. The fact of the matter is that any staff executive who is intelligent enough to manage an organization is intelligent enough to develop a strong and effective board.

The key to the development and maintenance of this delicate balance is the relationship between the chairperson of the board and the chief executive of the organization. These two individuals must build a firm trust-relationship. They must be able to "level" with each other, to discuss honestly and straightforwardly the issues before their organization. They must spend enough time together so that they are in agreement as to how the board and the chief executive are to work together. When problems arise with individual board volunteers, the board chairperson and the chief executive should be able to plan the strategy for resolution.

Agenda-building for meetings should also be an important part of their relationship. There should be agreement between them on all recommendations. If they cannot arrive at an agreement, the issue can still go before the board, with the clear understanding that the chairperson and the chief executive will be on opposing sides. Hopefully, such occasions will be infrequent and reserved for major issues. The condition of the delicate balance in a voluntary organization is directly related to the quality of the relationship between the chairperson of the board and the staff chief executive.

Staff must remember certain things which are important to their relationships with board volunteers. (Some of these are discussed in more detail in other chapters.)

First, and foremost, board volunteers involve themselves to help, not to take over or to interfere with operations. Board volunteers, just like staff, want to be successful in their roles. Interference or "takeover" doesn't fit into that frame of reference. Better understanding of each other breeds confidence. Confidence leads to trust.

Second, meaningful, clear, and accurate communication is the vehicle which moves staff and board volunteers from understanding through confidence, to trust, thereby allowing a close relationship without the loss of control or respect.

Third, staff should also keep in mind that the language of business and businesspeople is figures. Satisfy this language requirement first, and board volunteers can then relate to the program.

Fourth, board volunteers need to be able to predict the behavior of their staff, calling for such things as staff performance which keeps pace with promises, professional competence and personal integrity. They call for reasoned responses instead of a litany of "I think's" and opinions, and accurate data swiftly, and cheerfully supplied. Board volunteers don't expect their staff to be the best in the country; but they want them to be *among* the best.

Above all, staff must remember that working with boards is really the highest level of group work and that the same group dynamics are at work as in any other group. Personal victories for any one staff member, individual, or group will only lead to greater divisions. This does not sanctify consensus, but makes conflict-resolution such that no one loses face. After all, a prominent basketball coach once said that 82 percent of his games were won on rebounds.

The foregoing is essentially a discussion of the very role of staff: motivation of their board volunteers. Working in a voluntary organization is difficult and frustrating—with enormous rewards, if we are patient enough to nurture them. The succeeding chapters deal with some specifics of working with and structuring boards, such as writing bylaws and commissioning committees, and the selection, recruitment, orientation, training, and separation of board volunteers.

WHAT BOARD VOLUNTEERS BRING TO THE BOARD/STAFF RELATIONSHIP

Expertise in a variety of technical areas for which the organization couldn't pay.

The sanction of the various external publics.

Knowledge of various facts about the community.

Continuity of policy and program.

The ability to be a spokesperson.

Influence to attract financial resources, human resources, and public resources.

Preservation of the democratic process.

An objective point of view of operations; the capacity for critical review.

Ability to affect change in the organization.

Collective wisdom.

Exhibit 61

A final thought on the delicate balance: Much has been made of the relative status and power-differential between the board volunteer and the staff executive. The authors have heard the plaintive cry of the chief executive regarding his or her powerlessness to influence decisions, and "How can a person making a hundred thousand dollars a year respect one who is making fifteen thousand?" More often than not, however, when a staff executive's performance indicates that he could make a hundred thousand a year if he chose to, but that he has chosen instead to serve society at fifteen thousand, board volunteers will have the greatest respect for him. Real success is not measured in terms of dollars, but in terms of competency, respect, and stature in the lifework selected—*no matter what it is*. Strong boards and strong staff go together. It is a partnership which will lead to the achievement of the organization's goals.

Additional factors in maintaining the delicate balance are listed in exhibits 61–66.

WHAT BOARD VOLUNTEERS CAN REASONABLY EXPECT OF STAFF

Attention to details of meetings, conferences, etc.

Adequate preparation for meetings in which board volunteers must play a leadership role.

Complete, concise and accurate information.

Candor in individual and organizational relationships.

Judicious use of time.

Meeting of agreed-upon deadlines, with notification if deadlines cannot be met.

Prompt response to requests for information.

Prompt return of phone calls.

Exhibit 62

THIRTEEN EFFECTIVE WAYS TO
TURN OFF STAFF

1. Forget that staff members have the same feelings and emotions you do.

2. Treat your staff condescendingly.

3. Agree to a course of action privately, then change directions publicly without notifying staff of the reasons.

4. When meeting with a staff person, sign letters, answer many phone calls, dictate a letter to your secretary—all of these designed to demonstrate to staff how little you think of them or their time.

5. Communicate how busy you are to avoid a staff person's request for meeting.

6. Fail to achieve an agreed-upon task within the time frame allowed.

7. Step out of the board volunteer role into the staff role.

8. Once a deadline has passed, force staff to inquire repeatedly about progress.

9. Fail to recognize staff accomplishments.

10. Let a staff person know, in no uncertain terms, that you are doing him a favor by agreeing to a task.

11. Fail to return phone calls.

12. Put a staff person in a position of having to render an opinion about his colleagues or organization.

13. Instruct a staff person to do many hours of research or documentation without recognizing ongoing task loads or checking with his supervisor first.

Exhibit 63

WHAT STAFF BRING TO THE BOARD/STAFF RELATIONSHIP

Because of their unique position as the bridge between board and organization and between board members, staff can coordinate board activities and spot problems and pitfalls before board volunteers generally do.

In a culturally diverse organization, staff can be the bridge between cultures.

Objectivity in reaction to board volunteer suggestions.

Expertise in profession.

Basic knowledge of the organization.

Ability to interpret board policy decisions and actions to lower-echelon staff.

Exhibit 64

WHAT STAFF CAN REASONABLY EXPECT OF BOARD VOLUNTEERS

Fulfillment of commitments within agreed-upon deadlines.

Organizational knowledge and ability.

Candid performance appraisal and assistance in performance.

Leadership rather than "followership;" initiative rather than response.

Support in controversial situations.

Easy access by phone or visitation.

Sensitivity to staff's organizational problems.

Loyalty, confidentiality.

Exhibit 65

TWELVE EFFECTIVE WAYS TO TURN OFF BOARD VOLUNTEERS

Forget that board volunteers have the same feelings and emotions you do.

Ask for an appointment without saying what you want to talk about.

Forget that board volunteers are volunteers, not paid staff persons.

Fail to stick to appointment time schedules.

Don't ask board volunteers' advice or involve them in the decision-making process.

Forget to acknowledge board volunteers' accomplishments.

Have your secretary get board volunteers on the phone.

Embarrass a board volunteer through inaccurate or insufficient data.

Call a meeting with a board volunteer in your office.

Force a board volunteer to make repeated requests for data.

Send board volunteers form letters or letters with no signature.

Attempt to manipulate board volunteers in order to achieve a desired decision.

Exhibit 66

NOTES

1. © Copyright 1973 Charles W. Yost. Distributed by The Frye Syndicate, 2 Tudor City Place, New York, N. Y. 10017.
2. Charles A. Nelson, "Trusteeship Today," *Management Controls* (New York: Peat, Marwick, Mitchell and Co., May, 1972.)
3. Used with permission of Dr. Thomas R. Bennett II, president, Media Productions, Inc., P. O. Box 327, Downers Grove, Illinois, 60515.

THE BOARD MEETING

11

NOTE: This is an overview. For a more complete discussion on board meetings, see the Voluntary Management Press publication, "How to Conduct an Effective Board/Committee Meeting."

There are primary and secondary functions for board meetings. Unfortunately, most board meetings are based on the secondary functions. Primary functions must be accomplished *first*.

A board of directors has four primary functions:

1. To decide the planning framework.

2. To decide policy.

3. To implement certain policies.

4. To monitor (evaluate) policy implementation.

It would seem that the board meeting has two primary functions:

1. To decide policy.

2. To monitor policy implementation (both its own and policies delegated) from the following perspectives:

    A. Should it still be implemented?

    B. Should it be changed?

    C. What is the progress of implementation?

There are secondary purposes noted for board meetings, but they are by-products or conditions necessary for successful board meetings. Some of these are:

A social event: A board meeting is *not* a social event nor a place to "get to know each other," although sociability may be a by-product or important to success.

An educational meeting: Although education does take place, true education takes place outside of the board meeting.

Information/communication meeting: Although information and communication are integral to a good board meeting, it is not the primary place for either.

Inspirational meeting: Although inspiration takes place, a board meeting is not the best place for it. A reflective note or reference is fine but should be kept to a few words.

Board meetings *must* focus on its primary functions: policy-making and monitoring. The four by-products or conditions for successful meetings must be planned for separately, as the following questions illustrate.

1.   How do we provide for sociability?

2.   How do we provide for education?

3.   How do we provide for information and communication?

4.   How do we inspire?

Planning for these four should include the board meeting, but not using the board meeting as the primary place to deliver these four. Anything less will detract from the two essential functions of the board meeting:

1.   To decide policy.

2.   To monitor policy implementation.

Exhibit 67 illustrates the policy/monitoring cycle of an organization. Most policy decisions are made at the end of the current year for the following year. The first month of the fiscal period is used primarily to modify previous decisions.

Board of Directors Policy Cycle

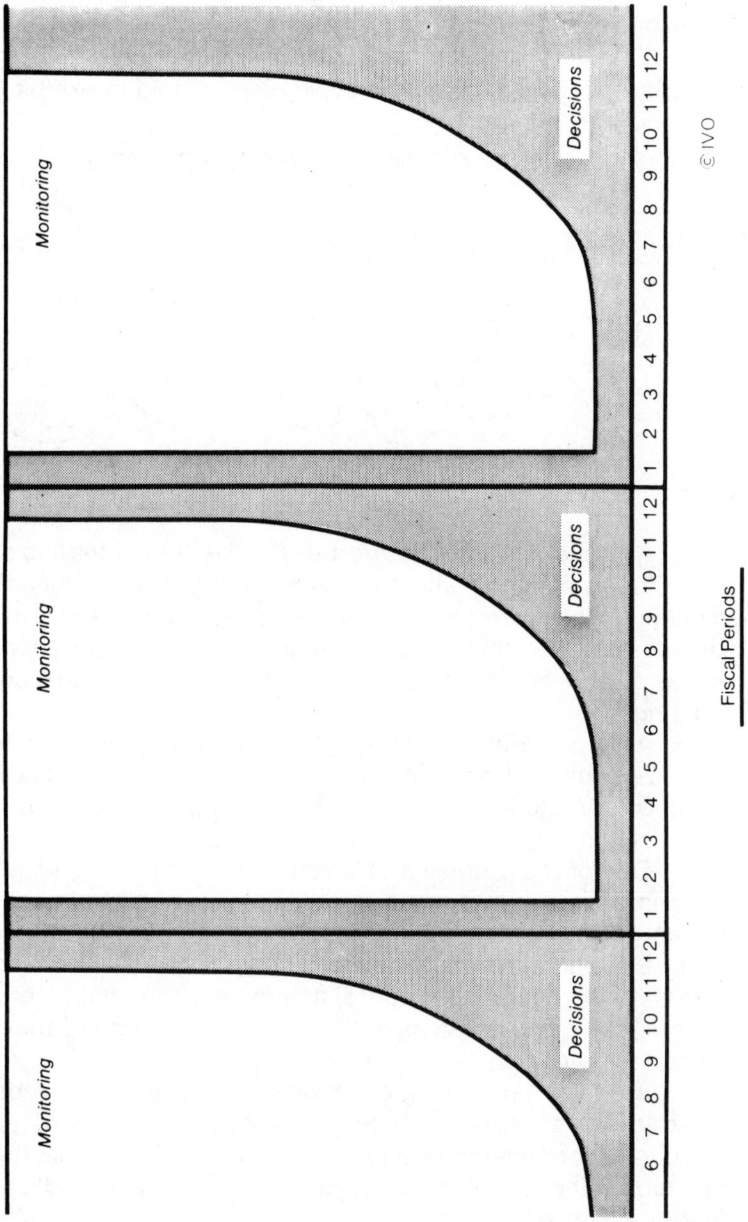

Monitoring

Decisions

Monitoring

Decisions

Monitoring

Decisions

1 2 3 4 5 6 7 8 9 10 11 12

1 2 3 4 5 6 7 8 9 10 11 12

6 7 8 9 10 11 12

Fiscal Periods

© IVO

Exhibit 67

Fiscal months 2–7 are primarily reserved for monitoring, with decisions escalating to the 11th and 12th months.

Voluntary organizations have too many board meetings. It is important to keep in mind the cycle diagrammed in exhibit 68.

BOARD-COMMITTEE MEETING CYCLE

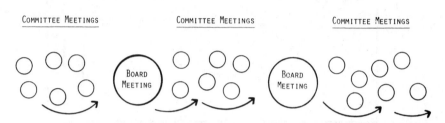

Exhibit 68

As a rule of thumb, if there are effective committee and executive committee meetings going on, board meetings need occur only four to six times a year, with quarterly meetings the minimum. Board meeting agendas flow from the work of committees and from current operating issues. Good board meetings, therefore, require good committee meetings.

As in committee meetings, the agenda and related data should be mailed out in advance of the meeting. See chapter 6, "The Role and Function of Committees," for the format to mail out advance material.

One of the problems of board and committee meetings is that assignments are made and accepted, then buried in minutes and forgotten.

Exhibit 69 is an easy way to keep track of issue flow and assignments. It can be used for board, committee, and staff meetings. The chairperson and staff member should each have copies to revise and make assignments.

A good board meeting can be a strong motivator. A bad board meeting—or a series of them—is deadly. With regard to newly-recruited board members, it is important to remember that this is their first look at the organization. Organizations cannot afford to have that first look tarnished.

Another point is that all boards should have a calendar. Exhibit 70 is a sample one.

NEWPORT ORGANIZATION

Board of Directors

Organizational Component

ISSUE FLOW AND ASSIGNMENT

Date

ISSUE	SOURCE	ASSIGNMENT	REPORTING PERSON	DUE DATE	ACTION REQUIRED
Poor handling of switch board	Public complaint	Staff Executive Director	Bob Johnson	-------	Resolve problem
No policy for use of bequests	Budget Committee	Business Committee	Tom Clark	May Board Meeting	Policy decision
Moisture entering west wing of bldg.	Staff to Building Committee	Property Committee to get bids	Joe Block	May Board Meeting	Decision on contract letting
Accounting proposal	Staff	Business Committee	Tom Clark	June Board Meeting	Policy decision
Interior painting schedule with costs	Board member	Property Comm. in consultation with Business Committee	Joe Block	Aug. Board Meeting	Approval to submit to Finance Committee
Issue 6	Property Committee	Business Committee	Tom Clark	Oct. Board Meeting	Decision for expenditure
Request for individual tutoring	Parents to staff	Program Committee	Juanita Perez	Oct. Board Meeting	Board approval
Report progress on Teen Center	Board member	Program Committee	Herman Dent	Nov. Board Meeting	Information only

Exhibit 69

NEWPORT ORGANIZATION

*BOARD CALENDAR FOR 19_*

MONTH	TASK	DATE
January or Fiscal Month #1	1. Budgets finalized for current year. 2. City-Wide meetings of Unit standing committee chairmen with corresponding Corporate committee chairmen. 3. Annual meeting	Jan. 7 Jan. 15 Jan. 20
February or Fiscal Month #2	1. General campaign kick-off. 2. General Report Meeting. 3. Boards of Managers Report Meeting. 4. Board of Directors Report Meeting.	Feb. 1 Feb. 15 Feb. 25 Feb. 28
March or Fiscal Month #3	1. General Report Meeting. 2. Boards of Managers Report Meeting. 3. Budget preparation kits distributed. 4. Board of Directors Report Meeting. 5. Executive Committee Meeting.	March 4 March 15 March 25 March 28 March 31
April or Fiscal Month #4	1. General Report Meeting. 2. Boards of Managers Report Managers. 3. Building inspection by Boards of Managers Property Committee. 4. Preparation of budgets. 5. Board of Directors Report Meeting. 6. Board Meeting.	April 5 April 15 April 20 April 25 April 28 April 30
May or Fiscal Month #5	1. Final General Report Meeting. 2. Boards of Managers Report Meeting. 3. Budget process continues. 4. Building inspection continued. 5. Board of Directors Report Meeting.	May 5 May 14 May 20 May 22 May 30

Exhibit 70a

June or Fiscal Month #6	1. Unit and Camp budgets approved by Boards of Managers and submitted to the Associate Executive Director.	June 6
	2. Executive Committee Meeting.	June 28
July or Fiscal Month #7	1. Budgets reviewed by Corporate Program Services Committee.	July 10
	2. Board Meeting.	July 25
August or Fiscal Month #8	1. Budgets reviewed by Corporate Reviewing Committee.	Aug. 10
September or Fiscal Month #9	1. Preliminary budget approval.	Sept. 15
	2. Financial Development Committees appoint Campaign Chairmen.	Sept. 20
	3. Nominating Committees elected.	Sept. 25
	4. Executive Committee Meeting.	Sept. 30
October or Fiscal Month #10	1. City-Wide planning meeting of all campaign chairmen.	Oct. 1
	2. Campaign chairmen recruit Corporate Division chairmen and Community Division chairmen.	Oct. 5
	3. Selection of team captains by campaign chairmen and division chairmen.	Oct. 15
	4. Board Meeting.	Oct. 20
November or Fiscal Month #11	1. Election of officers.	Nov. 8
	2. Divisional chairmen recruit team captains.	Nov. 15
December or Fiscal Month #12	1. Appointment of standing committee chairmen.	Dec. 10
	2. Meeting of team captains.	Dec. 15
	3. Executive Committee Meeting.	Dec. 18

Exhibit 70b

THE BOARD MEMBERSHIP PROCESS

12

The board membership process is the process of attracting board volunteers, deciding how they are to be treated, and, when necessary, how to separate them when they are not productive.

The crucial point in the board membership process is when the candidate is approached with "We need you!" The candidate usually responds: "What for?" *What for!* In the answer to this question lies the key to recruiting a board member, to an effective board, and, in the long term, to a successful voluntary organization.

Many conclusions can be drawn from the following statement and the two mini-plays; they illustrate a very narrow and self-destructive view of the board member.

> A board member is an unwanted necessity, recruited to do the vague and expected to do little.
>
> —A Staff Executive

Mini-Play No. 1:

Scene: A board meeting of a voluntary organization. During the meeting Joe Goodfriend waves his hand for the recognition of the board chairperson, Herman Easygoing.

Herman: Before we go on to the next item of business, let's see what Joe has on his mind.

Joe: Thanks, Herman. I've got with me Stanley Opportunist. Stan is a neighbor of mine—we've known each other for years. Last Sunday we were talking over cocktails and dinner. I happened to mention I was a member of this outstanding board and all the important people who belong. He thought it sounded interesting and wondered if he could join. I thought it was a great idea and brought Stan with me today. He's a good man, and our board could use him. I recommend him for membership. Let's vote on him.

Herman: Joe, a friend of yours is a friend of ours. All in favor of Stanley Opportunist for board membership say "aye." Opposed? Carried unanimously. Welcome to our board, Mr. Opportunist. Now the next item of business. . .

Mini-Play No. 2:

Scene: The office of George Munch, president of Ace Corporation. Mr. Munch is a member of the board of directors of the Hometown Organization and has been given the assignment of recruiting Lawrence S. Powerful, president of Powderpuff Industries. Mr. Munch's secretary has just reached Mr. Powerful by telephone:

Mr. Munch: Hi, Larry—quite a party you had last night! Thanks for the invitation. I meant to ask you, did you ever close that deal for Boodeen Company? . . . Fell through, huh? Too bad. Say, Larry, are you and Sally going to be able to join Viv and me at the Country Club dance next month? . . . Great! It's going to be a first-class affair. What did you decide about that boat? Are you going to get the six or eight sleeping capacity? . . . Sounds good. You should enjoy it . . . Sure, we'd like to cruise down to Florida. Let's clear our calendars and do it . . . Oh, you have a staff meeting in a few minutes. Look, this will only take a minute. You know I'm on the board of the Hometown Organization—would you care to join our board? . . . . No, it doesn't take a lot of time. Just a meeting once a month and none during the summer . . . No, there isn't much to do. Having your name associated with us will be a great help. . . What does the Hometown Organization do? Our big job is keeping the kids off the street—you know, keep 'em under close supervision and they won't be running around breaking windows and stealing . . . Good, I'll submit your name. . . Yes, I know you'll be too busy to come to any meetings for the next three or four months. . . Glad to have you aboard, Larry. See you tomorrow afternoon for a round of golf at the Club. 'Bye.

       *   *   *   *   *

The Board Membership Process

(An Ongoing Process)

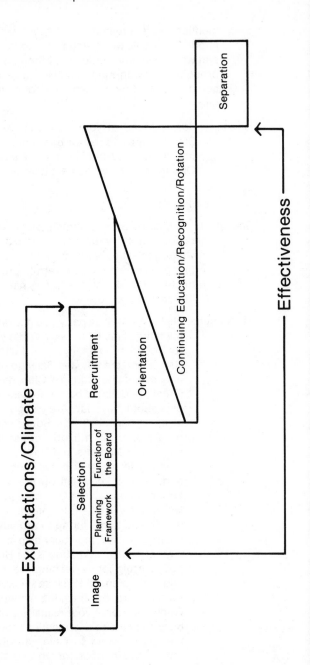

Exhibit 71

Exhibit 71 charts the board membership process, which is an ongoing activity. The image, selection, and recruitment phases will clarify what is expected of the candidate, and do much to establish the climate in which he/she will work. Orientation, continuing education, and recognition phases will determine the individual's effectiveness as a board volunteer and how he/she will react to before and after separation.

1. *Image*:   What the public thinks of the organization. A poor community image will make it virtually impossible to recruit key leadership.

2. *Selection*:   Careful scrutiny of candidates against agreed upon criteria.

3. *Recruitment*:   Putting together the best plan and personnel to persuade the candidate into serving on the board.

4. *Orientation*:   Recruitment is the introduction to orientation; where recruitment ends, orientation begins. In the recruitment phase, the board volunteer is given an overview of the organization. The orientation phase, on the other hand, is a more in-depth session. While the recruitment phase is concerned primarily with what the organization does, the orientation phase is concerned with *how* the organization functions.

5. *Continuing Education*:   Recruitment and orientation also include education. After orientation ceases, education continues for as long as the board volunteer remains. The education of a board volunteer includes both preparation for, and assistance in, executing his/her role.

6. *Recognition*:   Saying "thanks" for a job well done.

7. *Rotation*:   Rotating the board volunteer to different positions and committees within his/her tenure.

8. *Separation*:   The separation of a board volunteer through board action or through his/her own choice.

Within the board membership process, the committee responsibility is as follows:

Image:	Image Committee
Selection:	Board Membership Subcommittee

Recruitment:	Board Membership Subcommittee
Orientation:	Board Membership Subcommittee
Election:	Board of Directors
Continuing Education:	Board Membership Subcommittee
Rotation:	Board Membership Subcommittee
Separation:	Data Collection and Recommendation — Nominating — Action — Board of Directors

The board membership subcommittee of the resource development committee is a standing subcommittee because its activities are a year-round process. Because the nominating function is an event that takes place once a year, we recommend that a separate ad hoc nominating committee be formed to perform the following functions:

1. The evaluation of board members up for re-election, resulting in one of three decisions:

   a. Unqualified renomination—"A good board member."

   b. Programmed renomination—"Good potential, but we haven't found the key to greater involvement, so let's find a way."

   c. Programmed separation—A recommendation that the board member be asked to leave the board.

2. The nomination of officers.

The basic reason for separating the nominating committee function from the board membership committee function rests in the belief that a system of checks and balances will inhibit the growth of cliques or dynasties and will tend to keep as much bias as possible out of the evaluation process. To sum up this data: *Those who recruit should not also evaluate.*

See the Voluntary Management publication, "Nominating Committee Manual of Operation," for a full explanation of this committee's work.

We recommend that a board of directors be divided into thirds so that the terms of a third of the board volunteers expire each year. New board volunteers are elected to full three-year terms or to complete the unexpired terms of members who have left the board.

NOMINATING COMMITTEE

(AD HOC)

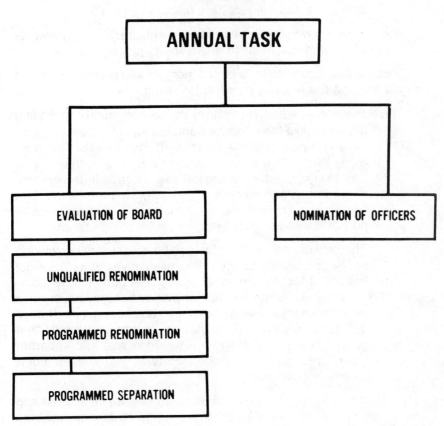

Exhibit 72

In a nominating committee meeting, committee members receive, for *each* board member up for nomination, a folder which contains such data as is necessary to evaluate that board member. Some qualifications for nominating committee members:

1. They are independent (not in the grip of the status-quo/ power element of the board). An elected nominating com-

mittee will probably have a somewhat better chance than an appointed one to escape such an influence.

2. They are sufficiently secure in their own professions, businesses and communities and are unafraid to objectively evaluate candidates.

3. They are well acquainted with the organization's goals and objectives and the resulting leadership needs.

4. They are well enough acquainted with the role requirements of a board volunteer to make sound judgments.

Some qualifications for a board membership committee would include the first three items, plus the following:

1. They have sufficient stature in the community to enable them to make the effective contacts that may be necessary to recruit new board volunteers. If they feel they have already "arrived" socially or in their businesses, they will be less likely, when selecting people, to substitute personal needs for the needs of the organization. In the case of urban voluntary organizations, it is important to have representation of the community sector on both committees.

2. They are of sufficient stature and have sufficient knowledge of the community to act as representatives of it. The most important fact to remember in the selection of either committee is: Although a prospective member may belong to a particular racial, ethnic, social, or business group, it does not automatically follow that he or she *represents* that group. There is a difference between real and apparent power; real power in a community is, many times, completely anonymous.

It is a continuing source of amazement how much evasion and downright dishonesty take place at the recruitment interview when the candidate asks, "What for?" Those who want a candidate for his money will deny it. If the candidate is expected to raise money, it is revealed only after he says "yes." The amount of time involved is described as "just a few meetings." Those who want only the candidate's name will emphasize a function he can serve.

The obvious question is: Why deceit—for that is what it is—when candor will better serve the candidate and the organization. Are we afraid to tell people what we are and that it takes *work* to be a good board member? Or is it that those who recruit are as ignorant of the truth as is the candidate? Are staff executives afraid to "level"? Are they afraid of building strong boards? Regardless of any fears, recruiting must be, above all, *honest*. It is just as important to get a "no" as it is to get a "yes."

Nature of People

Before discussing the seven phases of the board membership process, a few words need to be said about the nature of people. In the first chapter of his book, *Designs for Fund-Raising* (New York: McGraw-Hill, 1966), Harold J. Seymour did an outstanding job with this subject, and the authors urge the reading of this book in full. What follows is a summary of that chapter in capsulized form:

Four kinds of people:

1. 5 percent—leaders, initiators, creators.
2. 25-30 percent—responsible; will do what they say they will do.
3. 45-50 percent—responsive; will respond to pressure.
4. 20 percent—inert fifth.

Universal aspirations:

1. To be "sought."
2. To be a worthwhile member of a worthwhile group.

What people tend to do:

1. To strive for measurable and praiseworthy attainment.
2. To seek or achieve unity by group action.
3. To act only under the pressure of a deadline.
4. To relish earned reward and recognition.
5. To repeat pleasurable experiences and to avoid unpleasant ones.
6. To conceal unpraiseworthy attitudes.
7. To lose our sense of community, with more mobility and greater numbers.
8. To give incomplete attention and, indeed, to shorten the attention period itself.

9. To glance, instead of read.

10. To admire excellence, but to suspect perfection.

11. To generalize from acceptable fragments.

12. To respond to the warmth of good sentiment.

13. To prefer incomplete exposure—even a little mystery.

14. To like a due amount of dignity in the images of their leaders.

15. To take the message somewhat obliquely.

16. To go for grooves, categories and easy formulas.

17. To reject concepts of debt.

18. To suspect and resist change in itself, or any other implied threat to security.

19. To go with the winning horse.

20. To pay attention and devote interest in direct proportion to personal identification.

21. To revere the past, deprecate the present and fear the future.

Why do people join boards? If today's boards are going to be as diverse as they need to be, we have to know a bit about "why" a board volunteer joins and what his or her needs are. Staff and other board volunteers must not make value judgments about a candidate's reasons for joining.

These concepts apply to *all* board volunteers, regardless of socio-economic considerations. The following three charts illustrate a few basic concepts of the "why" of board membership.

People join boards to satisfy needs, as illustrated on the right side [of exhibit 73]. The eight items are meant to be representative, not exhaustive. The point is that we do not make judgments on the reasons for joining a board; we simply recognize that they are *there* and that an individual's willingness to accept boardservice demands rests, in large measure, on his/her reasons for joining the board in the first place. Increased response to boardservice demands is brought about through a board volunteer's *involvement* (left side of chart).

We must look at need satisfaction. On the left side [of exhibit 74] are three reasons for joining a board; they tend to be *growth-*

Need Satisfaction

Board Service Demands	Company Requirement Asked by Peer Assigned by Boss Business Connection Recognition-Status-Prestige Identification with Cause Community Service Something to Offer
Involvement	Non Value-Judgment

Exhibit 73

facilitating. In other words, at the outset, there exists a personal climate conducive to increased involvement and productivity.

The right side of the chart lists five reasons for joining a board. These tend to be *static.* Individuals who join for any of these reasons tend to remain at the same level of minimal involvement.

The secret of increased commitment is to move individuals into

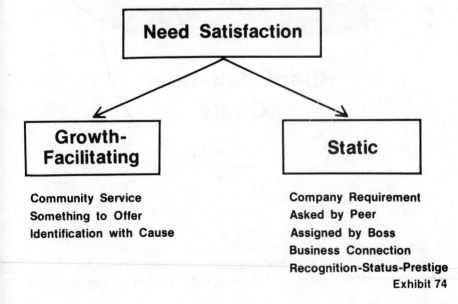

Growth-Facilitating	Static

Growth-Facilitating	Static
Community Service Something to Offer Identification with Cause	Company Requirement Asked by Peer Assigned by Boss Business Connection Recognition-Status-Prestige

Exhibit 74

a growth-facilitating stance. The board membership process is a guide for this.

Some organizational theory suggests that the greater the goal integration within an organization, the greater the satisfaction and the smoother the operation. This theory is illustrated by the three over-lapping circles [in exhibit 75]. Increased communication is the key to increasing goal integration.

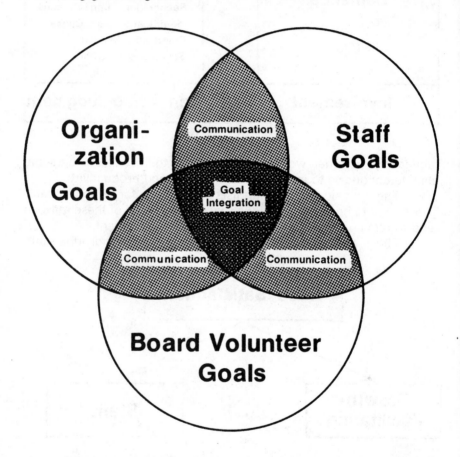

Exhibit 75

Of course, goal integration is never total, nor should it be. Never-theless, some degree of goal integration is needed.

A board never fully matures until it can identify with the organi-zation's cause or purpose. It is their *commitment* which causes board volunteers to move outside themselves to what Lord Moulton called "obedience to the unenforceable."

Phases of the Board Membership Process

I. *IMAGE*

A candidate for board membership is judging the organization before the recruitment interview even begins. He or she will have some conception of the organization from radio, television, local units, comments from his/her peers, subordinates and superiors, newspapers, magazines, the organization's literature, and other publicity media. Because of a particular circumstance, or series of circumstances, his/her conception may range anywhere from a vague impression to a thoroughly hardened opinion. This is called image—and one of three conditions generally exists:

Positive: The organization is well known and respected.

Neutral: Not much is known about the organization or it is entirely unknown.

Negative: The organization has a poor public image through unfavorable incidents or inadequate facilities, staff, programs, and support.

Recruitment is simplified by a positive image. It becomes more difficult, with considerable persuasion required when a neutral image exists. It is practically impossible when a negative image exists.

Image is a composite of public relations and publicity. Publicity is the program the organization generates to create a favorable impression in the community, such as radio and television spots, billboards, posters, newspaper articles and ads, magazine articles and ads, and, community involvement.

Public relations is what the public thinks about the organization after the public comes in contact with a piece of publicity. Board volunteers, staff, and clients are all public relations agents. A million dollars in publicity can be lost by one poorly handled phone call or contribution. Exhibit 76 illustrates this important concept:

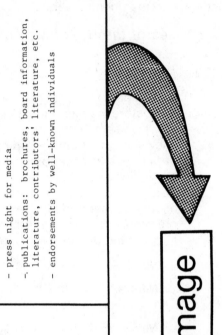

PUBLICITY

The communication of information, the pursuit of attention and interest through appeals to eye and ear, and sometimes visibility for its own sake.

- media: TV, radio, newspapers, magazines
- billboards
- public transportation displays
- public building displays
- press night for media
- publications: brochures, board information, literature, contributors' literature, etc.
- endorsements by well-known individuals

PUBLIC RELATIONS

The influence of an infinite number of tremendous trifles:

- how phones are answered
- timing and tone of replies to mail
- attitude toward complaints
- service to constituency
- reception of visitors
- follow-through on commitments
- public appearances by board volunteers, clients, staff, etc.
- "feelings" of publics
- thoughtfulness and sensitivity
- recognition
- good information flow

Image

B62-2-78

Exhibit 76

II. *SELECTION*

Too often, the first step in the board membership process is "Whom do we want?" The result is a list of names of people with the rather vague comment, "He or she will do a lot for us!" The "lot" is never defined nor is there any guarantee he or she will *do* the "lot." The first question is not "who," but "why." Unless there are well-defined criteria of the work to be accomplished by the board of directors, there is no way to intelligently recruit an individual. To provide the "why," two things are required:

> *A Planning Framework:* This is the framework that describes what policies need to be decided upon and what work is to be done by the board.
>
> *The Board Function:* This specifically describes the function of the board within the planning framework and the role of the individual as a part of the board.

There are two considerations in candidate selection:

A. *Personal Considerations*

1. Does he/she have stature in the community?

2. Does he/she have interest?

3. Does he/she have leadership potential?

4. Does he/she have communication skills?

5. Is he/she available?

6. Does he/she have affluence and/or influence?

7. What are his/her spheres of influence?

8. Does he/she have integrity?

9. Is he/she successful in his/her own field?

B. *Knowledge and Skills*

These must be matched to the requirements of the board. Exhibit 77 is a useful form in determining the criteria for knowledge and skills required for board membership. The criteria at the top are only an example of what can be devel-

NEWPORT ORGANIZATION	YEARS ON BOARD	AGE				SEX		RACE OR ETHNIC					SANCTION								
		21 - 35	36 - 50	51 - 65	Over 65	Male	Female	(Relevant to community)	Latin	Black	American Indian	Oriental	Neighborhood	Law Enforcement	Education	Political	Corporate	Churches	Local Media	Small Businesses	Medical
BOARD COMPOSITION ANALYSIS																					
BOARD VOLUNTEER																					

	RESOURCE DEVELOPMENT							POLICY DETERMINATION														
								PROGRAMS					BUSINESS		RESOURCE DEV.					PERSONNEL			
Personal wealth	Access to corporations	Access to individuals with money	Willing to give proportionate to means	Willing to raise money	Willing to contribute services	Willing to make material contributions	Education	Health and PE	Counseling	Group Work	Arts	Vocational	Budgeting/Fiscal Control	Property Management	Capital Giving	Planned Giving	Annual Giving	Recruitment of Board Membership	Image	Wage & Salary Admin.	Performance Appraisal	Fringe Benefits	Personnel Policy

© IVO

Exhibit 77

oped by an organization to match their board requirements. The exercise for preparation of this form is:

1.   The board of directors commissions the resource development committee to recommend a format. The work is done by the board membership subcommittee.

2.   The board membership subcommittee reports to the board with a suggested format.

3.   Once approved, the committee places the names of the board volunteers down the left side and makes check marks in the appropriate boxes. By adding up the check marks at the bottom of the columns, requirements for new volunteers should be clear.

Once this form is shared with the board, it is possible for the board to suggest candidates based on these criteria.

Following are additional considerations for the optimum:

Politics	*Education*	*Health*
Republican	A.B.	Good
Democrat	M.S.	Poor
Independent	Doctorate	
Liberal	Professional	
Conservative	None	

Wealth (Net Worth)	*Religion*
$1,000,000 plus	Roman Catholic
$500,000 to $1,000,000	Jewish
$250,000 to $500,000	Protestant (all denominations)
$100,000 to $250,000	Other
Under $100,000	

Annual Income	
$1,000,000	$25,000 to $49,000
$500,000 to $1,000,000	$10,000 to $24,000
$100,000 to $500,000	Under $10,000
$50,000 to $99,000	Unknown

Exhibit 78 is a format for a candidate form for present board volunteers, to be submitted to the board membership sub-committee.

NEWPORT ORGANIZATION

CANDIDATE FOR BOARD MEMBERSHIP

(Prepared by the Sponsoring Member of the Board of Directors)

Name: _____

Address (Business): _____ Tel. _____

(Home): _____ Tel. _____

Occupation & Position: _____

Education and/or Training: _____

_____

Honors: _____

Organizations: _____

_____

Charitable Activities in which he/she is *actively* engaged: _____

_____

What are his/her current interests in the Newport Organization? ___

_____

What activities would particularly interest him/her? _____

_____

_____

Willing to engage in fund raising? _____

Your personal recommendation: _____

_____

_____

Sponsor: _____

Date: _____

Exhibit 78

III. *RECRUITMENT*

After a candidate is selected, the next phase of the board membership process is the recruitment phase. The first step is to put together the recruitment plan, based on knowledge of the candidate, and to select the most effective personnel to persuade the candidate to undertake board service. Remember that the recruitment phase dwells more on *what* the organization does, while orientation concerns *how* the organization does it. In a meeting of the candidate, the recruiting board member, and the staff executive, the following points should be considered:

A. Estimating Time Requirements of Board Membership

   1. Active Board Participation—Three to six hours monthly. This includes:

      a. Board meetings

      b. Committee meetings

      c. Fund raising

      d. Meetings with staff

      e. Telephone calls

         This varies according to the time of year (summers are light) and the activities scheduled (fund raising is heavy from October to April).

   2. Leadership Responsibilities—An additional two to four hours monthly. This includes assuming such positions as:

      a. Board chairperson

      b. Other board officers

      c. Committee chairperson

      d. Campaign chairperson

      e. Campaign vice-chairperson

      f. Campaign team captain

      g. Representing board at other organization functions.

B. The recruiter then gives the candidate "Your Invitation to Service" (Voluntary Management Press publication), or its equivalent. (The kit is presented at the end of the interview.)

The staff executive discusses the first three sections with the candidate:

1. What the organization does—material in "Service" publication, slides, films or flip charts.

2. How the organization is organized.

3. Budget.

C. The board volunteer discusses the function and role of the board volunteer and the function and role of the staff.

D. At this time, the candidate is informed of the specific committee for which he/she is being recruited. Because the work of the board is done through committees, it seems appropriate to assign a candidate at the outset. This issue is further discussed under the topic of *Rotation.*

E. Before a candidate officially assents to having his/her name placed for election, many organizations are asking candidates to go through orientation. Sometimes a candidate will agree to recruitment, but change his/her mind after orientation. It is better to have them drop out at the outset rather than to become deadwood later.

G. Follow-up

1. A letter from the chairperson of the board informing the candidate of his/her election.

2. A letter of welcome from the staff chief executive.

3. A letter from the chairperson of his/her selected committee containing the following:

a. Welcome to the board and to his/her committee

b. Committee commission

        c. Minutes of the past several committee and board meetings

        d. Request for an appointment to get acquainted and for orientation (followed by a phone call)

4. A letter of welcome from the campaign chairperson containing the following:

        a. Welcome to the board

        b. Campaign job in current years

        c. Campaign structure

        d. His/her team assignment

5. A letter from the campaign team-captain containing the following:

        a. Welcome to the board

        b. Request for visit to discuss campaign role

6. Publicity releases should go to:

        a. Metro media

        b. New board volunteer's home community newspaper

        c. New board volunteer's company newsletter

        d. New board volunteer's trade, professional or other associational newspapers and magazines

7. A board volunteer's confidential information sheet is sent out. See exhibit 79.

Exhibit 80 is a checklist for the staff chief executive to follow.

IV. *ORIENTATION*

As stated in the previous section, the recruitment phase is designed to give the prospective board volunteer an overview of *what* the organization *does.* The orientation phase is designed to give the prospective board volunteer (or new board volunteer) a much broader perspective—*how* the organization does its work.

The objective is to bring the board volunteer to a productive work level as soon as possible. The orientation should have two parts:

General: This is the overall functioning of the organization.

Committee: As stated in *III: Recruitment,* a board volunteer should be recruited to a committee.

In a time frame, one-half to two-thirds of the orientation should be general, and the balance committee.

A.   General Orientation

This should be done by staff and board volunteers concerned with the phases of orientation, coordinated with the executive director or his/her designate, such as the director of resource development, associate or assistant executive director, etc.

The orientation should follow the management divisions. A prospective or new board volunteer should receive a three-ring binder, empty except for five dividers or tabs: one each for administration, business, personnel, resource development, and program services. As an individual moves through orientation, appropriate material can be added to each section. At completion, the new board volunteer then has a complete manual of operation. Exhibit 81 is a sample orientation form showing orientation flow and assignments.

B.   Committee Orientation

This orientation should be conducted by the committee chairperson or his/her committee designate and the staff person assigned to the committee. Some topics for this phase:

1. The committee commission

2. Samples of activities of the committee for the previous twelve-month period

3. The committee minutes for the previous twelve-month period

NEWPORT ORGANIZATION

BOARD VOLUNTEER INFORMATION

(CONFIDENTIAL)

NAME: _____BIRTH DATE: (Day & Month) _____

ADDRESS: _____TELEPHONE: _____

_____ ZIP CODE:_____DATE ELECTED TO BOARD: _____

NAME OF SPOUSE: _____BIRTH DATE: (Day & Month) _____

NUMBER OF CHILDREN: DAUGHTERS_____ SONS_____

EDUCATION: (College attended and type of degree or degrees received)

_____

_____

_____

_____

FRATERNITY MEMBERSHIP: _____

_____

MEMBERSHIP IN ASSOCIATIONS, SERVICE CLUBS, SOCIAL
            CLUBS: (Include offices held and committees served on)

_____

_____

_____

_____

POLITICAL OFFICES HELD: _____

_____

_____

_____

Exhibit 79a

CIVIC APPOINTMENTS HELD: _____

_____

_____

_____

MEMBERSHIP IN OTHER VOLUNTARY ORGANIZATIONS: (Include
offices held and committees served on)

_____

_____

_____

_____

REFERRED FOR BOARD MEMBERSHIP BY:_____

_____

RECRUITED TO THE BOARD BY:_____

_____

ARE YOU AVAILABLE FOR: TV Shows_____ Radio Programs_____

HOBBIES AND SPECIAL INTERESTS: _____

_____

_____

_____

For publicity purposes, please send a photograph.
If you do not have one, we would like, with your
permission, to send a photographer to take one.

Please return to:

Company _____

Address _____

_____

Phone _____

Exhibit 79b

NEWPORT ORGANIZATION

STAFF EXECUTIVE'S CHECK LIST FOR NEW BOARD VOLUNTEERS

NAME _____ACCEPTED ON _____

		CHECK LIST	COMPLETED
1.		Personal History File Folder Prepared	
2.		Board of Directors Individual Contribution Record prepared (see page 6 of the Voluntary Management Press publication, *Nominating Committee Manual of Operation*)	
3.		Board Volunteer Personal Data	Mailed	
			Received	
			Follow Up	
4.		Photograph received	
5.		Letter of Welcome from executive director	
6.		Letter of Welcome from Chairperson of the Board with carbon copy to Executive Director	
7.		Letter of Welcome from Chairperson of Committee with carbon copies to chairperson of Board and Executive Director	
8.		Letter from Campaign Chairperson	
9.		Visit from Campaign Team Captain	
10.		Orientation Session Set Up	
11.		Metro News Release Sent	
12.		Local News Release Sent	
13.		Company House Organ Release	

Exhibit 80

   4. If available, a meeting schedule and the agenda and date
      of the next meeting

A new board volunteer will feel considerably more comfortable when the first assignment involves understanding
and participating in the committee assignment. A sense of
participation and achievement is always greatest in a small
sphere of work that is closest to the volunteer's own skills
and knowledge. The broader organizational understanding
comes later.

The best way is to have a board/staff team doing the orientation for several people at once. However, since people
tend to join boards at different times, it makes little sense to

NEWPORT ORGANIZATION

Orientation for _____ SALLY E. JONES _____ Date _____

Committee Assignment _____ PERSONNEL _____

ITEM	TIME	PLACE	STAFF/BD.	PICK UP TIME & PLACE
1. Site visit	2 hrs.	Unit I & II	Exec. Dir.	Exec. pick up at SEJ's Off. 10 a.m. 10/12
2. Administration —Structure—Bd. & Staff —Role & Function of Bd. & Staff. —Planning Program	1 hr.	SEJ's Off.	Board Chr. & Exec. Dir.	At SEJ's Off. 2 p.m. 10/14
3. Program Services	1 hr.	Adm. Off.	Pro. Dir. & Chr. of P.S. Comm.	Will come at Noon 10/18
4. Resource Development —Support —Image —Volunteers	1 hr.	Adm. Off.	Dir. of Res. Dev., Chr. of R.D. Comm.	Will come at 10 a.m. 10/20
5. Business —Budget —Property —Investment	1 hr.	Adm. Off.	Dir. of Business	Will come at 1 p.m. 10/21
6. Personnel	3 hrs.	Adm. Off.	Dir. of Personnel	Will come at 1 p.m. 10/21
TOTAL TIME	9 hrs.			

Exhibit 81

delay an orientation until there are four or five people ready. There have been organizations that hold to a strict time-table. Board volunteers may receive orientation programs after already serving six to eight months.

Orientation should be held within a week of recruitment and depend on the candidate's schedule. Some will give the whole period in one block of time; others tend to segment it as illustrated in exhibit 81. However orientation is done, it must be done well.

We recommend that a prospect not be permitted to say "yes" to standing for election until after orientation. Orientation becomes another screen. It is possible that a prospect may say yes to recruitment and "no" after orientation. As stated previously, it is better to detach deadwood as early as possible.

If a prospect refuses orientation, it is doubtful the prospect would have been a good board volunteer anyway.

V. *CONTINUING EDUCATION*

Recruitment, orientation, and continuing education overlap. When a prospect is being recruited, the individual is, in a sense, being oriented and is receiving an education.

Once the prospect says "yes" or "no" to recruitment, the recruitment phase ends. If the prospect says yes, he/she will move into orientation. After orientation is concluded, the new board volunteer participates in continuing education for the entire period of his/her board service.

Basically, there are two types of continuing education— formal and informal:

> *Formal:* This type includes the programs or meetings which are specifically set up for continuing education purposes.

> *Informal:* This type involves continuing education that is not specifically planned but takes place within the framework of processes, meetings, and programs set up for purposes other than continuing education.

Some examples:

A. Formal

1. Sessions conducted by the organization or taking part in administrative or program topics such as effective boards, new programs, present or projected legislation, site visitation, etc. See exhibits 82 and 83.

2. A communications network such as newsletters, board and committee minutes, human interest stories, and newspaper articles.

NEWPORT ORGANIZATION

ONE DAY CONFERENCE ON BOARDS

Purpose: 1. To provide orientation to Board Organization and Board Membership.

2. To provide a forum for the exchange of ideas and concerns between Corporate and Unit Boards.

James L. Curtis
Conference Chairperson

11:00 a.m.	Registration
11:30 a.m.	Luncheon—Monroe Room
12:30 p.m.	General Session—The Voluntary Concept

Presiding: James L. Curtis, Chairperson
                     Resource Development Committee

Public Relations   Herbert Lunn, Chairperson
Program: Public Relations Committee

Speaker: Eliott P. Sampson, Chairperson
                     Newport Organization
                     "The Organization of the Newport Organization"

Split Sessions on Standing Committee Purpose and Function

1:00-1:45 p.m.   *Room A—Program Services Committee
                   Chairperson: Herman S. Schmidt*

1:50-2:35 p.m.   *Room B—Resource Development Committee
                   Chairperson: Lloyd M. Tully*

2:55-3:40 p.m.   *Room C—Business Committee
                   Chairperson: William C. Pierce*

3:45-4:30 p.m.   *Room D—Personnel Committee
                   Chairperson: Rodney T. Pratt*

Each Color Group will have a 45 minute session with each Standing Committee. There will be a 20 minute coffee break at 2:35 p.m.

Color groups will move as follows:

Red   A — B — C — D
Blue   B — C — D — A
Green   C — D — A — B
Purple   D — A — B — C

4:40-5:20   *Wrap-Up Panel to Respond to Questions of Conferees—Monroe Room
             Closing Remarks—Eliott P. Sampson*

5:30 p.m.   *Cocktails (Cash Bar)—Monroe Room*

Exhibit 82

NEWPORT ORGANIZATION

CONFERENCE ON BOARDS

"Conceptual Consistency/Operational Diversity"

Date: May 28, 29, 30, 19__
Place: Newport Country Club

1st Day, May 28—Concepts and Framework

10:00 a.m.	*Opening Remarks*
10:15-12:00	*The Board Survey*
12:30 p.m.	*Lunch*
2:00-4:00 p.m.	*The Voluntary Concept*
	1. Components of Voluntary Organization
	2. Role and Function of the Staff
	3. Board Structure
	4. Role and Function of the Board Volunteer
	5. Board Policy Process and Policy Implementation
	6. Involvement/Contribution Ratio
	7. The Delicate Balance
4:00-5:00 p.m.	*Board Volunteers as Clients*
5:00-6:00 p.m.	*Diagnosis and Action*
6:30 p.m.	*Supper*

2nd Day, May 29—Nuts and Bolts

9:00-11:00 a.m.	*The Mythology and Methodology of the Staff Role*
10:30 a.m.	*Coffee and Rolls*
11:30-12:00	*The Organization of the Newport Organization*
	1. The Board of Directors
	2. Parallel Organization of Boards of Managers
	3. Board/Staff Relationships and Accountability
	4. The Bylaws
12:00 noon	*Lunch*
1:30-3:00 p.m.	*Board and Committee Relationships*
	1. The Committee Commission
	2. Make-up of Board and Committees
	3. Ad-Hoc Committees
	4. Agenda Building
	5. Meetings
	6. Minutes
3:00-3:15 p.m.	*Break*
3:15-5:30 p.m.	*Newport Organization Committee Commissions and Making Them Work*
5:30-6:30 p.m.	*Diagnosis and Action*
7:00 p.m.	*Supper*

3rd Day, May 30—Diagnosis and Action

8:00-10:00 a.m.	*The Board Membership Process*
10:00-10:15	*Break*
10:15-12:30	*Diagnosis and Action*
12:30 p.m.	*Closing Remarks*
3:00 p.m.	*Check-Out Time*

Exhibit 83

3. Sessions conducted *outside* the organization which are attended by board volunteers.

B.   Informal

1. Committee and board meetings are designed to conduct the work of the board, but they are also a powerful informal continuing education force.

2. The interrelationships of board volunteers between

—themselves

—staff

—clients

—community

must also be recognized as powerful, informal continuing education forces. The formal continuing education processes are vital because they directly affect the informal type. The less data available from the formal network, the more the informal network thrives on *misinformation, misconceptions, misrepresentations and mischief.*

The four M's cannot be completely isolated. However, an effective continuing education program can substantially reduce their damage.

Finally, although not strictly a part of continuing education, it is vital to an organization that a climate of "belongingness" for board volunteers be established. The continuing education process is extremely important in this respect too.

Also important is the knowledge staff has of board volunteers and how well they use it to demonstrate that staff consider them more than instruments. Little things such as an occasional thank you note for work done or congratulations on some special occasion such as a promotion or birthday are examples of such motivation. Staff must *know* their board volunteers.

As members of an organization, we ask board volunteers for their help; then we tend to whitewash problems for them, do their work for them (if it gets done at all), do their thinking for them (as if they were *non compos mentis*), feed them a steady diet of baffling and/or dull statistics (as if we believe they wouldn't understand the really important issues), and, avoid all controversy in meetings (lest we learn something both from and about them, or have our own pet ideas challenged). So, in addition to keeping them for life, we do all we can to make it a life of starvation, stagnation, and suffocation. Continuing education is the key to avoiding this situation.

VI.   *RECOGNITION*

Board members are on the board for a variety of reasons. As stated earlier, however, for whatever reason a person joins a board, he/she is still human and likes to have his/her efforts recognized. Recognition may be given in several different *forms*: by presenting him/her with an award such as a plaque or certificate, and/or, informally, with a thank you letter or simple words of praise at a board meeting. The *reasons* for recognition range from contributions of money to contributions of time and effort. The *sources* of recognition are the board itself, members of the organization, the community, the national organization, and others. However it is handled, recognition must take place and be given consideration from three points of view: form, reason, and source.

CAUTION: Sometimes in the rush to recognize, awards are given to too many people for a multitude of reasons. There is a delicate balance in recognition: just enough to give everyone the opportunity to be justly recognized for work well done, but not too much to cause recognition to lose value.

These are the formal, organizational types of recognition. Don't ignore the informal, such as noted at the end of the continuing education section. Sometimes, the unexpected, thoughtful, and small "remembrances" by staff, clients, or fellow board volunteers are as effective, or more effective, than the formal ones.

The Kimball Foundation produces "Thank-U-Grams." These are very useful in recognizing good works. Request samples of Thank-U-Grams from:

Kimball Foundation
24 Northcote Drive
St. Louis, Missouri 63144

VII. *ROTATION*

There are four rotational possibilities:

A. The first refers to rotation within, not off, the board. It has been suggested that new board volunteers be assigned to a committee, matching their knowledge and skill to the knowledge and skill required on the committee. After two years of successful service, a board volunteer should be much more knowledgeable of the organization. At that time, the board volunteer could be offered the opportunity to serve on a different committee.

B. Service on ad hoc committees is possible. Board volunteers could be asked to serve on ad hocs while temporarily suspending work on their standing committee assignments.

C. Rotate leadership positions. Allow different people to assume different chairpersonships.

D. Board volunteers could be asked to serve on committees outside of the organization or to represent the organization through speeches, meetings, and television and radio appearances. These add the elements of fun and recognition to board membership.

VIII. *SEPARATION*

Inevitably, there comes a time when a board volunteer will leave for any of the following reasons:

Voluntary—Resigns because of ill health, business transfer, promotion, lack of time, or disenchantment.

Involuntary—Is asked to resign from the board.

Death

There are many organizations which have a bylaw provision which states that no one may serve more than two consecutive terms. This usually is a painless way of dropping unwanted board volunteers. Unfortunately, the organization then scrambles to construct frameworks to keep a relationship with "good" board volunteers.

If the recruitment and orientation programs are well done,

and if it is common knowledge that board volunteers' performances will be evaluated, then mechanical means of separation are generally not required. It is far better that continued or discontinued board service be based on performance than on mechanics.

In the few cases in which an individual must be asked to resign, one or two board volunteers should call on the individual, commiserate about how busy he/she is, and suggest that because of the changing conditions, he/she may not care to stand for re-election.

In the even smaller number of cases in which the individual does not take the hint, then he/she must be told that there really is no choice. The point is to make the separation as amicable as possible. A friend is wanted, not an enemy.

These are the eight phases of the board membership process. Do them well and the chances for an effective and efficient board of directors are greatly enhanced. All that has come before in this chapter can be summed up in this statement by a former, productive board volunteer:

"Don't expect what you don't ask for!"

COMMUNICATION

13

"I know you believe you understand what you think I said, but I'm not sure you realize that what you heard is not what I meant."

The problem of communication in a voluntary organization is complex —especially when the board of directors occupies the position it does in the decision making or policy process. There are three primary communication issues which must be considered:

1. The inter-personal communications between individuals

2. Inter-board and intra-board communications

3. Communications between the board and its publics

This chapter will not deal definitively with these three areas; the purpose here is to highlight the issues.

1. *The inter-personal communication between individuals.*

Exhibit 84 shows communication viewed rather simply.

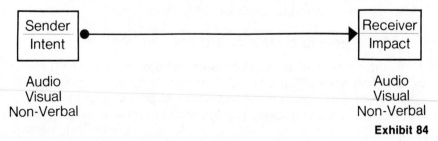

Sender	
Intent	

Receiver	
Impact	

Audio
Visual
Non-Verbal

Audio
Visual
Non-Verbal

Exhibit 84

Unless the sender is extremely careful how he/she communicates, the impact could be very different from the intent. There are many types of variables:

1. The written word can be misinterpreted.

2. The spoken word can be correct, but the nonverbal communication can undercut what is spoken.

3. Visuals, such as graphics, can convey one message; the spoken word another; and the non-verbal, a third.

4. Cultural differences can cause considerable difficulties; what is considered culturally correct to one can be culturally anathema to another.

There are other variables; these are merely illustrative. To make the illustration complete, a feedback line must be added, as in exhibit 85.

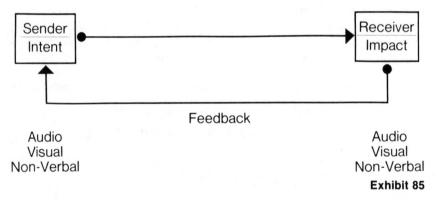

Feedback

Audio   Audio
Visual   Visual
Non-Verbal   Non-Verbal

Exhibit 85

It is only through carefully constructed feedback processes that we can be sure of the impact of our intent. Much time is spent in the first phase of communication to the practical exclusion of the second phase: Feedback. If more consideration were given to feedback, much of the communication problem would be eliminated.

2.   *Inter- and intra-board communications.*

Inter-board—A system of communication among board members is imperative. Often, so much time and effort are expended on the communications between the board and its publics that the *internal* mechanisms are overlooked. It is important to have well-constructed board and committee meetings and concise, articulately written communications, such as minutes of meetings and newsletters. There should be ample opportunity for small groups of board members to meet and work on specific tasks. Limited communications tend to narrow the decision-making process to a few people. The board then becomes an oligarchy.

Intra-board—If the organization is a multi-unit one and the governing board has established unit boards to oversee the operations of the units, there may develop a different kind of communication problem. At the corporate level, it is quite simple to make decisions which affect the local units without the participation of these units. The lawful authority to decide exists but the wisdom of exercising such authority without consultation is questionable.

Unit boards should be represented on all committees—standing, sub, and ad hoc—which affect their destiny. This includes voting membership on the governing board. (See chapter 6.)

3. *Communications between the board and its publics.*

A board of directors has these publics: administration, administrative staff, line staff, and clients. The names vary as the organization varies, but the problem remains the same: If a board of directors has the ultimate authority, how does it receive and interpret information to make those decisions? There are three basic systems of communication between the board and its publics (see exhibits 86–88).

The chain of command system has advantages: It is efficient and swift. Information is filtered before reaching the board. Some meetings can be dispensed with. It has, however, two major problems. One, it gives the staff chief executive great power; for he is the main "dispenser" of information. What the board hears, essentially, is what the executive wants it to hear. Two, the board has little or no contact with its publics, which are represented through the administration. The whole effect is a very restricted perception of operations on the part of the board.

The open system has the decided advantage of open communications; everyone has direct access to the board. It also gives the board a much better perspective of what is going on in the organization. In addition, it affords the publics of the board an opportunity to participate in the processes of the organization.

It has one major disadvantage, however. An enormous amount of time is required to implement such an open system. To maintain it

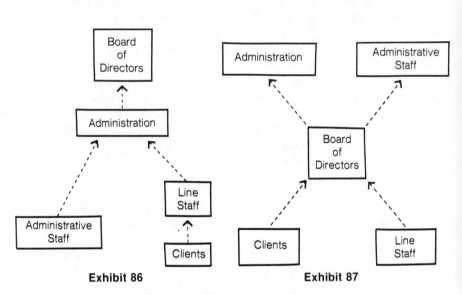

Chain of Command

Open System

Exhibit 86

Exhibit 87

requires longer meetings, in which everyone has the opportunity to speak. Moreover, individual board members can be the recipients of unlimited attempts at lobbying and endless complaints.

The open chain of command is preferred by the authors. It provides the best features of both the chain of command and the open systems. The board's publics can participate in the data-gathering process through participation on the various committees. This provides firsthand data for the board and great experience for the non-board participants.

Any requests for policy change or other decision-making should go through the chain of command. Administrative staff, line staff, and clients who wish to have policy or decisions heard by the board must go through the chain-of-command side.

For this system to be effective, it should be made policy and understood by everyone. Any deviation from it should be avoided, as exceptions will destroy the value of the system.

Whatever system is used, the communication issue is illustrated in exhibits 89 and 90, the *communications network*. Exhibit 89 shows the voluntary organization at the center of the network—sending and receiving information to the public. Exhibit 90 illustrates another network in existence. Here the publics communicate with each other, and the voluntary organization is excluded.

Open Chain of Command

(Chain of Command)
Policy Consideration

(Open)
Data Gathering
Communication

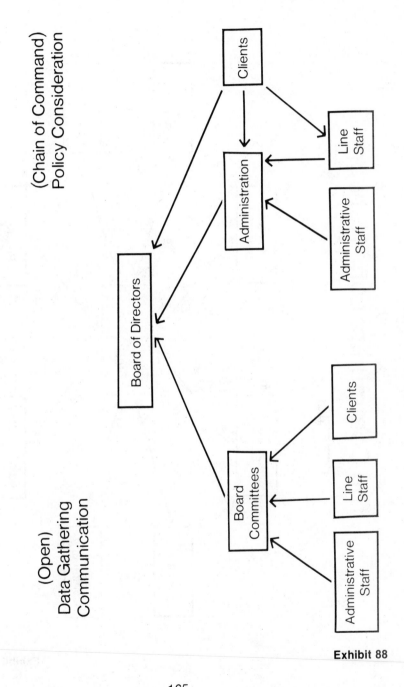

165

Exhibit 88

The Communications Network

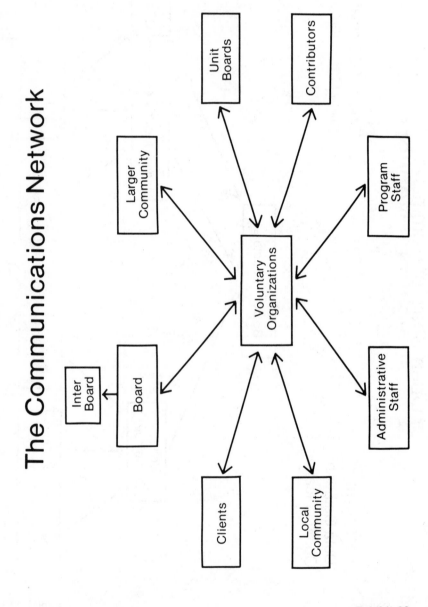

Exhibit 89

The Communications Network

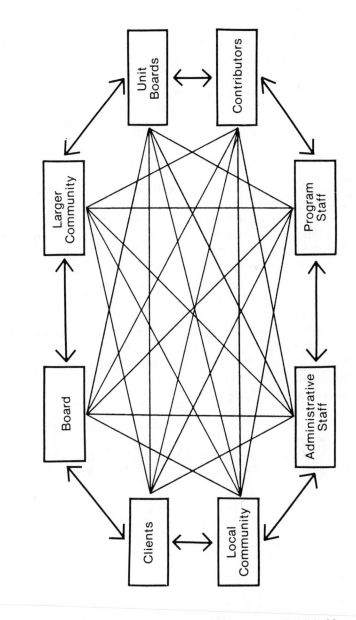

Unit Boards ↔ Contributors

Larger Community

Board

Program Staff

Administrative Staff

Clients ↔ Local Community

Exhibit 90

The significance of these two networks is apparent when the voluntary organization sends out different messages to different publics, according to what it believes each particular public wishes to know. The folly, of course, is that the publics do talk among themselves. If they find out different information has been sent to each, organizational credibility is lost.

A final note on communication concerns *information flow.* Any staff member must understand and know the difference between:

1.   The need-to-know for decision making

2.   The need-to-know for climate

The need-to-know in order to make a decision can be very narrow, usually restricted to a series of facts that lead to a logical conclusion. This type of need-to-know reduces the decision-making process to the level of mechanics. It likewise tends to constrict the thinking of those who have to make decisions to the tangible, the logical.

The need-to-know for climate is more humanistic. This kind of data brings the decision-making process into human terms and stirs the emotions of the recipient, producing a sense of belonging and involvement.

Information limited to the need-to-know for decision making can only cause organizations to become impersonal and result-oriented, at the expense of people. Information for climate, on the other hand, produces the environment in which decision making can more realistically take place.

Knowledge without common sense is folly; without method, it is waste; without kindness, it is fanaticism; without religion, it is death. But with common sense, it is wisdom; with method, it is power; with charity, it is beneficence; with religion, it is virtue and life and peace.

(Author unknown)

DIFFERENT TYPES OF BOARDS AND CULTURALLY DIVERSE VOLUNTARY ORGANIZATIONS

14

Boards of all types pervade our society in almost infinite variety. They are found in the corporate world, in government, in not-for-profit organizations, in social clubs, and so on. As they vary in type, they also vary in their effectiveness. Some are used extremely well, while others are there in name only, to meet some legal requirement.

Despite their variety, and however they are labeled, there are only two basic types of boards:

1. *Governing boards*—Their function is to control and assist.

2. *Advisory boards* —Their function is to provide assistance; they have no power to make policy decisions.

We have placed this discussion of the various types of boards at the end of the book because we wish to emphasize that, although boards may differ in what they do, they are quite similar in *how* they do it. With little variation, the concepts and practices discussed throughout this book apply with equal force to both governing and advisory boards.

Governing Board

A governing board has the *legal* responsibility and authority for the organization it serves. An advisory board gives advice to some other authority. There are two types of governing boards:

1. Self perpetuating—This type of board fills its own vacancies and goes on year after year.

2. Membership elected—(This board is illustrated by exhibit 91.) Membership elects the board of directors at an interval mandated by the bylaws. The board of directors may fill vacancies as they occur, but they, along with the board, must be elected by the membership at the membership meeting, usually on an annual basis.

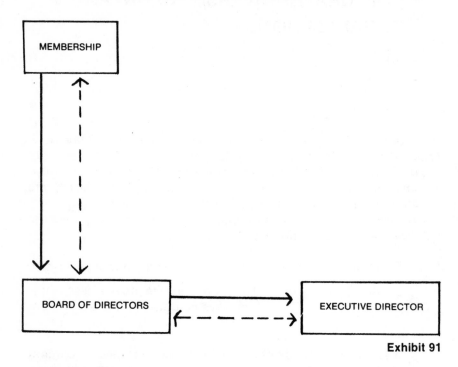

Exhibit 91

Advisory Boards

Governing boards often appoint ancillary boards—women's boards, men's boards, associate boards, etc.—to carry out specific functions such as fund raising, or special programs. These ancillary boards frequently hold a prominent place in the life of an organization, but do not have the governing powers of the board which appointed them.

However, governing boards should be careful in their use of the word "board." Board connotes authority. We believe that, when possible, a governing board should have no other boards except in the case of unit boards. Other boards in an organization often assume power they are not entitled to.

If a board or committee appoints advisory groups, the guidelines need to be as specific as they are for governing boards. Exhibit 92 gives some guidelines for advisory groups.

Regardless of the type of board, the individuals who serve on them require careful nurturing. One must resist the temptation to devote full energy and time to the governing board at the expense of the supporting boards. An organization may have both types of boards throughout, and they should be treated equally.

Culturally Diverse Voluntary Organizations

Within the types of board, there is the problem of culturally diverse voluntary organizations. In the last ten years, two factions arose and are still causing problems: The first is one that was introduced under the "sanction role" of a board member. That is, community people are demanding a voice in the institutions which affect their lives. This demand was supported by the "War on Poverty" administration by the Office of Economic Opportunity under President Johnson. The second is that minority staff members rightfully expect to assume more and more positions of authority in their organizations. The white, upper and middle class Anglo-Saxon majority is no longer able to control the urban voluntary organization—on either the board or the staff side.

Two primary areas of conflict arose from these new conditions in culturally diverse voluntary organizations. The first returns us again to the subject of the sanction role of board volunteers. Culturally diverse voluntary organizations found that community people could readily close the doors of the organization by simply withdrawing the constituency. This meant a new and frightening element was added to the development of a board. Community people sat down with corporate people to manage the institution, and, for the first time, those of absolutely different races, cultures, classes, and degrees of power were brought face to face.

Dan H. Fenn, Jr., of the Harvard Business School, distinguishes this new condition by referring to the organization as both "traditional" and "contemporary." "Traditional" refers to the establishment-type, while "contemporary" includes the recipients of the service rendered.[1] Because of the volatile nature of contemporary boards, Mr. Fenn points out that business people are far more comfortable in the traditional setting.

The second area of conflict revolves around the staff executive. As more minorities and members of ethnic groups assume executive

ADVISORY GROUP COMMISSION

TO: Advisory Group

FROM: (Appointing Authority)

General Commission

The Advisory Group is commissioned by and responsible to (*Appointing Authority or Another Group or Individual*).

(A general statement of the purpose of the Advisory Group should follow. The length of time the group is to exist should be included.)

Appointments and Composition

This section should answer the following questions:

1.   How is the chairperson selected?

2.   How are members selected? Number to be selected?

3.   What is the length of service of the group?

4.   What are the criteria for selection?

Age	Special groups
Race or ethnic group	Members of the organization
Community representative	Other

5.   Requirements for recruitment and orientation.

Responsibilities

A clear statement of responsibilities should be written for each of the four functions. Delete any functions not applicable.

1.   Advice

2.   Advice and implementation

3.   Own programs

4.   Support to appointing authority

Also included in this section should be the frequency of meetings expected.

Exhibit 92

positions, they find themselves in the unusual position of trying to find a balance between the community groups with whom they identify (the "contemporary") and the corporate groups they need to financially maintain their organization (the "traditional"). The reverse, of course, is true of the majority staff executive in a minority organization.

In discussing this problem with a number of staff executives and board volunteers in urban voluntary organizations, it is clear that "culture" has been the point of difference, the element which is necessary to understand in order to comprehend the dynamics of an urban voluntary organization. The following four exhibits have been created to illustrate graphically this role of culture.

A culturally common voluntary organization is one in which in general—repeat, *in general*—board volunteers, clients, and staff are of the same cultural background. Disagree as they may on policies and procedures, at least their deliberations are unclouded by cultural considerations.

A Culturally Common Voluntary

Organization

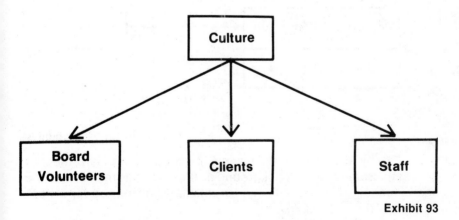

Exhibit 93

An entirely different situation is found in a culturally diverse voluntary organization. Exhibit 94 shows one of two possible conditions which may exist. In this case, the board is composed of both corporate (larger community) and community (local community) people. If members of the staff are from the same cultural background as their clients and the community people of their board, they may experience difficulty in relating to the corporate side of the board. The result is that the staff tries to overload the board with community members, generates a fear of corporate people, and creates an unbalanced organization. Or, it is also possible that this staff member may overcompensate in his attempt to identify with the corporate side of the board, accepting their values over his own values, his/her profession, and the issues of his/her clients.

A Culturally Diverse Voluntary Organization

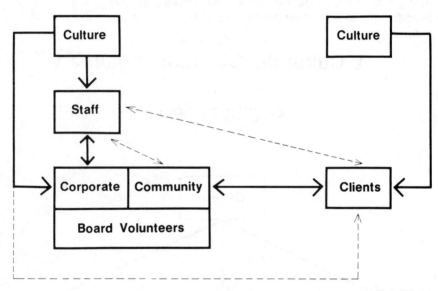

Exhibit 94

Exhibit 95 illustrates the reverse of this condition. Here, the staff is from the same cultural background as the corporate members of the board, resulting in communication problems which may be opposite to those found in exhibit 94.

Considering all these situations, a very natural question might be asked: "How on earth does a culturally diverse voluntary organization manage—when confronted with differences in culture, status, power and commitment—to resolve conflicts between board member and board member, between staff and board?" There is no easy answer

A Culturally Diverse Voluntary Organization

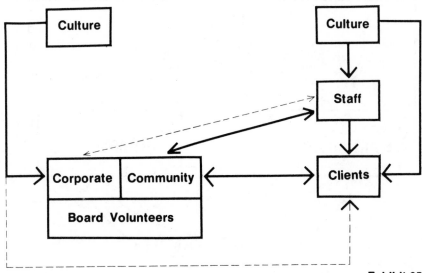

Exhibit 95

to such a profound question. Exhibit 96, however, suggests at least the framework for an answer.

Exhibit 96 illustrates the fact that there is a great deal of participation by the local community in the decision-making process of the organization, but a small amount of contribution income. On the larger community side the participation is equally great, with the voting power equally shared, but with this side bringing in most of the dollars. A working relationship between these two groups must be built on mutual trust and need—a condition known in biology as "symbiosis" (two dissimilar organisms living together in a mutually beneficial association) with the staff serving as the symbiotic agent, the element which enables this condition to thrive. The latter has great significance for the education and training of staff who must serve in culturally diverse voluntary organizations. Another point which needs underscoring is that the basic concepts of a voluntary organization are not invalidated in an urban surrounding; but the mechanics used to implement those concepts must be adapted.

Mr. Arthur J. Bell, director of the General Robert E. Wood Unit of the Chicago Boys' Clubs, is an effective professional who has assisted his club, his board, and his community in coping with the difficult

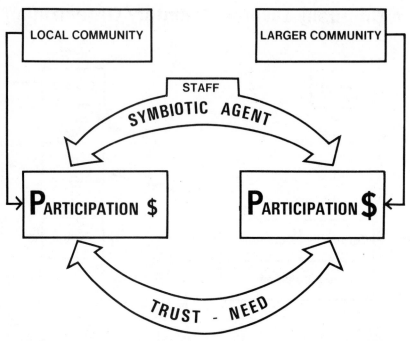

Exhibit 96

transition from a Polish and Bohemian community to a Mexican-American one. He wrote the following case study and the questions which accompany it—an excellent piece of work which ties together the many elements of working with a culturally diverse voluntary organization.

BOARD—BUT NEVER BORED

The Caesar Chavez Boys' Club—former George Washington Unit—is located in a "Latino barrio" of a large city. The community was formerly made up of Swedish, Norwegian, and a few Dutch people. The annual budget of this club is one hundred fifty-thousand dollars. The board raised eighty-five thousand last year; the balance was derived by allocation from the Community Fund.

Andy Brown, club director, felt a shot of adrenalin surge to his breast as he picked up the semi-weekly issue of the *Rosewood Reporter*, local community newspaper. Right on the front page was a picture of a group of people carrying picket signs and dumping garbage on a suburban lawn. The signs seemed to indicate that the people were unhappy with the kind of service they were getting from their landlord, and they were, therefore, taking their complaints directly to him—where he lived. This kind of thing was happening somewhere in the city almost every day, but the Boys' Club had never before been involved.

The headline of the paper blared: CHICANOS MARCH ON SLUM-LORD. The story and pictures went on to tell how a group of Latinos had assembled at the Caesar Chavez Boys' Club—garbage in hand—and proceeded to a western suburb, where they deposited it on the lawn of a resident who owned a building near the Club. Although the article did not state directly that the group had been organized by the Club, the several references to the Club clearly implied that it had at least sanctioned the action. Andy was sure he had not heard the last of this.

Before he had time to plan his strategy, Juan Garcia appeared in his office. Mr. Garcia was one of the chief organizers of the demonstration, a recently-elected community board member, and a member of the Program Committee. Mr. Garcia felt that, as a member of this committee, it was necessary to spend a portion of each day checking up on the program; and, since his appointment, his big attendance record at the Club had been second only to that of Andy Brown. His self-appointed duties included challenging everyone in the junior gamesroom to ping pong, "helping" to coach soccer, and mediating fights. His usual solution to the latter problem was to tell the boys involved that they should "go to the gym, put on the gloves, and settle it the right way."

The reason for his appearance this morning was soon very obvious. "What kind of prejudiced idiots do you have working around here, anyway? Last night, when you were off, I stopped in the Club after my 'visit to the suburbs.' That Black guy you've got running the gamesroom was really manhandling one of *our* kids. It's not bad enough our kids get pushed around in school by them—they've even got to catch it at their own Club! Let me tell you something, Andy, the people in the barrio are getting tired of getting the short end from both the Blacks and the Anglos. I know you think I'm spying on your staff, but some board member has to know what's going on around here. Those high-class, big-shot gringos wouldn't think of looking in on the program on their own time. Besides, they probably think that some 'wetback' will do them in if they come down here after dark."

Before Andy had a chance to respond to Mr. Garcia, his board chairman, William C. Rockway, came charging through the door like a cannon-shot. "Well, well," he said, "if it isn't my favorite social worker and my favorite garbage man! What are you two guys going to do—go out and sprinkle tamales on the lawns of the rest of the Board? I'm sure our men will be waiting in line to work on the finance campaign when they see what you two guys and the Mexican Mafia did to me last night."

"A lot of us have about had it with this place. We went along with dropping off the name of the Father of Our Country and changing it to that of a grape-picker. We agreed to put a bunch of do-nothings on the board of directors just so we could have some local color. Why, this hot-shot group raised only two-thirds of their thousand-dollar goal. If you had to count on them to raise your salary, you'd be eating pinto beans out of a clay pot. The garbage on my lawn last night was bad enough, but the last straw was when my next-door neighbor presented me with a little souvenir that had rolled up on his lawn—and do you know what was stenciled on the inside? I'll show you."

With this, he tossed a garbage-can cover on Andy's desk. Andy didn't even have to look down to read the message. About two weeks ago, the janitor had painted on every garbage can and cover: "Taken from the Caesar Chavez Boys' Club." Just then, an elderly gent stuck his head through the doorway and said in a heavy Swedish accent: "Andy, if you're not too busy entertaining the more influential people, would you take a look at the boiler? Our Golden Age Club is really cold up there, and since two of us are now board members, too, if you don't make it hot for us, we'll make it hot for you—ho-ho-ho!"

Discussion Questions:

1.   List the problems.

2.   For each problem listed, try to:

   a. Tell how it might have been avoided.

   b. Tell what should be done now.

3.   Is there any one major problem that seems to underlie all the rest?

4.   What are some resources you would use to solve these problems if you were director of the Chavez Boys' Club?

5.   What kind of training should the club director have in order to cope with these problems?

*   *   *   *   *

The following are a few points that staff might well keep in mind as they attempt their symbiotic role:

1.   Careful orientation and training of corporate board volunteers.

2.   Careful orientation and training of community people; answer their question: "Why me?"

3.   Don't limit community people to serving only on the program services committee and its sub-committees. Community people can be excellent on budget reviews; they

can count, and they are good money-managers—with respect to fund raising.

4. Even the poorest community can raise a little money. There is something stirring about Mrs. Jones's reporting on progress toward the five thousand dollar goal of the community phase of the campaign. The issue is not giving, but *proportionate* giving. Mrs. Jones's five dollars is just as real as Mr. Smith's five hundred. Communities can raise money in lots of ways: bazaars, pancake days, rummage sales, luncheons, dinners, door-to-door solicitation, ad books for community businesses, raffles, bake sales, and so forth. Community people, doing their part *proportionately*, will stir corporate people and motivate them.

5. Break down the membership community into two components: corporate and community, with joint meetings.

6. Try to bring in some of the younger corporate people who can adjust to the new urban voluntary organization more easily than the older, establishment types.

7. Rotate board and committee meetings between afternoons and evenings. If afternoon, make arrangements with a community member's employer for time off without jeopardy. Such arrangements can be made either through the professional or through other board members. Point out to community people that transportation to and from meetings, meals, and other items essential to organization business are tax deductible.

8. Community people will tend to want action on *immediate* problems, although they also expect something to be accomplished toward eradicating the causes of the problems. Corporate people, on the other hand, are more prone to look at the underlying cause of a problem and apply a long-range process to its solution. After all, the immediate problem doesn't affect them, and they can afford to take time to study it. A balance needs to be struck somewhere between these two positions.

9. In the social spectrum of the urban board, it must be remembered that membership in a given group—racial, ethnic, or socio-economic—does not necessarily confer upon the member a valid right to represent it. In other

words, a vocal group member may command much attention and come across as representing the entire group
when, in reality, he speaks only for himself. Staff must be
extremely careful to distinguish between intimate knowledge of the organizational structure of the community.

10.   Another problem which can arise in the urban board has to
do with the causes for a particular community concern. An
example of this type of problem occurred on an urban
board when members of the community became concerned about a deteriorating apartment dwelling that was
threatening the health and welfare of its residents. Seem-
ingly, nothing could be done. After some investigation,
however, it came to light that the owner of the building was
a member of that same board. Other similar situations can
appear.

A word about the great opportunity of the culturally diverse
voluntary organization: In chapter 1, it was stated that many of the
most influential people in the country hold membership on someone's
board, giving the staff a unique opportunity to effect changes in
society. A businessperson's service on a culturally diverse and properly developed board can be an eye-opening education for him or her
into the world of urban problems. If we combine education and social
conscience, a powerful force for change emerges. Here again, our
hope resides in the young, up-coming businesspeople who will be tomorrow's leaders. If they can be brought into tune with the problems
of urban areas, they will then be in a position to redress those problems
at their source, rather than just "buying a hundred rat-traps."

Staff must, therefore, broaden its idea of service to clients so
that it includes the board volunteers. Through service to clients, staff
members are preparing their clients for society; through service to
board volunteers, they can prepare society for their clients. The whole
idea may be summed up this way: "The action of one on behalf of
another—performed in the interest of both—is *service*."

A quote from John W. Gardner seems particularly appropos at
this point because of its implications for the culturally diverse voluntary organization:

No society will successfully resolve its internal conflicts if its only asset
is cleverness in the management of these conflicts. It must also have
compelling goals that are shared by conflicting parties; and it must have
a sense of movement toward these goals. All conflicting groups must

have a vision that lifts their minds and spirits above the tensions of the moment.[2]

Saul Alinsky also provided a revealing insight into problems of the culturally diverse voluntary organization when he blamed much failure in communication on a lack of "even the most elementary grasp of the fundamental idea that one communicates within the experience of his audience—and gives full respect to the other's values."[3]

NOTES

1. Dan H. Fenn, Jr., "Executives as Community Volunteers" *Harvard Business Review*, March-April 1971.
2. John W. Gardner, *Excellence* (New York: Perennial Library, Harper and Row, 1961), p. 139.
3. Saul D. Alinsky, *Rules for Radicals* (New York: Random House, 1971), p. xviii.

WHAT DO I DO NOW?
OR HOW TO USE THIS BOOK*
15

If you are an Executive Director . . .

you must work with your board chairperson and/or other key board volunteers. Share the book and work with them to establish an ad hoc committee to plan the process of change.

If you are a Board Volunteer . . .

start with your executive director. Plan with him/her how to bring about change.

By the streets of "By and By," one arrives at the House of "Never."

—Cervantes

What a board does—or does not do—is the result of the collective behavior of individual board volunteers. If we can affect the behavior of individual board volunteers in the performance of their roles, then the board of directors automatically achieves its function: assuring the continued viability of the voluntary organization managed by that board of directors.

Imagine a football game where the field is marked out, goal posts erected, a football placed at the fifty yard line and 22 players lined up. The officials blow a whistle and say, "Play ball!"

---

*Material in this chapter is from the Voluntary Management Press publication, "GUTS—Get Underway, Try Something."

There is a condition—there are no rules. Confusion and frustration reign as players are told they must win the game and the game has not been made clear. In the ensuing chaos, officials are helpless because they too do not know the game nor its rules.

Although the analogy is not exact, we many times do the same thing to the boards of directors and staffs of voluntary organizations. Because the statutes call for a board of directors, we have one. What we do not have is the rule book for its operation.

Without the rule book, or framework as we call it, individual board volunteers and staff "do their own thing," rendering collective action, if taken at all, irrelevant or dominated by either board or staff or a few individuals of either or both sides.

The situation is further complicated by the wide diversity of board function in other organizations. A board volunteer can serve on five boards of directors and receive five completely different viewpoints of what a board is and how it should function.

This book can form the basis for an organization to establish a conceptual framework of a board of directors upon which to base operational processes and procedures.

Recognize concepts.
Mechanics will follow.

One approach to building a board/staff consensus on a board concept is to conduct a seminar for board and staff members.

The seminar should cover concepts and practical processes, procedures, and structure. Out of this an organization must design its own concepts and the processes, procedures, and structure that are the "mechanics." Committees cannot be established until there is a management concept, and policy cannot be determined until there is a concept of planning.

If the behavior of a board reflects the behavior of board volunteers and staff, then the focus of improvement or change must be on the individual and the organizational climate and structure that affects that behavior. The issue, then, is competency. We need competent individuals, board and staff, to manage the affairs of the organization. As John W. Gardner says, if we are to have self-renewing organizations, we must have self-renewing individuals.

Exhibit 97 shows a cycle useful in planning for continuous renewal.

STEP 1	Establish ideal model for board and individual behavior.
STEP 2	Measure your organization's position relative to the ideal model's.
STEP 3	Analyze and interpret your organization's position against the ideal model. Prepare diagnosis through a force field analysis.
STEP 4	Based on the diagnosis, prepare a plan of action taking into account concept, structure, roles, behavior of individuals, climate, etc.
STEP 5	ACTION Get Underway, Try Something!

Exhibit 97

STEP 1   Establish ideal model for board and individual behavior.

A seminar is designed to permit an organization to establish the ideal board model. The full board and staff should take the seminar. Usually, the IVO-sponsored seminar is attended by one or more board volunteers, staff or a combination. Following their participation, arrangements should be made for full board and staff participation.

STEP 2   Measure your organization's position relative to the ideal model's.

The *Survey on Boards* is designed to measure the conceptual foundation of board and staff. The self assessment for *Voluntary Governing Boards of Directors* is designed to measure the operational position of the board. Both these publications are from Voluntary Management Press.

STEP 3   Analyze and interpret your organization's position against the ideal model. Prepare diagnosis through a force field analysis.

A force field analysis is designed to identify the forces that tend to limit the movement from a given situation and those that tend to facilitate movement. It begins by establishing a clear action goal. Exhibit 98 is a model.

ACTION GOAL: "To broaden and intensify board volunteer participation and involvement."

LIMITING FORCES

↓ ↓ ↓ ↓ ↓

————————————————————————————————— PRESENT SITUATION

↑ ↑ ↑ ↑ ↑

FACILITATING FORCES
(STRENGTHS)

OPPOSITE OF GOAL: An inactive, uninvolved board.

Exhibit 98

The following are steps designed to use the force field analysis as a diagnostic tool on which to base a plan of action:

1. Identify forces at work. These forces can come from the seminar materials, or from your organization situation. The following are examples of possible forces. Keep in mind that these forces can be either limiting or facilitating—or they can be new, brought in to bolster the facilitating:

Committee structure

Committee commissions

Job descriptions for board volunteers

Board meetings

Agenda building

Role of staff

Role of the board volunteers

Trust

Organizational planning

Data preparation for board and committee meetings

Policy and implementation

Board-membership process—selection, recruitment, orientation, continuing education, rotation, separation

Bylaws

Rotation of officers and committee chairmen

Evaluation of board volunteers

Program involvement

Publicity and public relations (image)

Training of board volunteers

Training of staff

Relevant programs

Staff feelings about working with boards

The seminar

Board chairperson

Committee chairperson

Decision-making process

2.   In exhibit 99, review and list on the left side those forces which tend to be facilitating.

3.   In exhibit 99, review and list on the right side those forces which tend to be limiting.

4.   In exhibit 100, review and list what forces can be added to the facilitating side.

5.   Any implementation is not without consequences. In checkers, a move is not made without trying to ascertain in advance the consequences of that move. So it is with planning; the greater our ability to predict problems the less chance that problems and crises will appear down the road.

In exhibit 101, list the predictable consequences of your implementation and how those consequences affect your plan and what you have to do about it.

FORCES AFFECTING ACTION GOAL IMPLEMENTATION

FORCES . . .	
. . .TENDING TO BE FACILITATING:	. . . TENDING TO BE LIMITING:

Exhibit 99

WHAT NEW FORCES CAN BE ADDED TO THE FACILITATING SIDE?	

Exhibit 100

CONSEQUENCE:	HOW THIS AFFECTS OUR PLAN AND WHAT WE HAVE TO DO ABOUT IT:
1.	1.

Exhibit 101

One consequence of increased board-volunteer participation and involvement is that this will require considerably more staff time and involvement.

STEP 4   Based on the diagnosis, prepare a plan of action taking into account concept, structure, roles, behavior of individuals, climate, etc.

The forces are objectives. Use exhibit 102 to list the objectives requiring action.

Use exhibit 103 to list targets required to implement. Voluntary Management publications *So Now You Are A Chairperson!* and *How To Conduct A Board Meeting* are useful in implementing the plan.

STEP 5   ACTION
                Get Underway, Try Something!

Before moving to Step 5, review the following to be certain they have been considered in arriving at Step 5:

1.   Have you focused your objectives on *causes* rather than *effects*? Structure, planning, and the board membership process are the *causes* for good or poor motivation, functioning or nonfunctioning committees.

     If causes are improved, effects will follow. Focusing on effects may provide short-term benefits, but will only yield long-term crises.

2.   Move to your Ideal Board Model gradually. Make moves only commensurate with the competency of your board and staff to move comfortably. Vital: leadership must have followership.

3.   Do not impose change. Involve those whose behavior must be modified in the change to a better functioning board. Assist them to understand that the new way is better for them *and* the organization.

4.   Change is emotional because it can and does threaten individual security. Understand this. Deal with it rationally, using objective and impersonal data.

5.   If the board is to be improved, it begins with the board chairperson and the staff chief executive *wanting* it to improve.

OBJECTIVES WORK SHEET

DATE PREPARED: _____

SEQUENCE	OBJECTIVES	ACCOUNTABILITY	START-UP DATE	COMPLETION DATE

Exhibit 102

TARGETS WORK SHEET

OBJECTIVE # _____ :_____

_____

DATE PREPARED: _____

SEQUENCE	TARGET	ACCOUNTABILITY	START-UP DATE	COMPLETION DATE

Exhibit 103

A board improvement plan has a greater possibility of success if these two support and work together towards improvement.

6. Finally, returning to step 1, desired improvements will take place within the ideal model established, and as the organizational climate becomes conducive to change.

It makes for a good football game!

RESISTANCE TO CHANGE

I couldn't understand why other folks feel
that an idea of mine is no good;
I couldn't understand why they hem and they haw
when I tell them to do what they should.

I couldn't understand why they seem to feel
that their own ideas meet the test;
but when others suggest an improvement to make;
they claim that the old way is best.

One day I asked a wise old man
why nearly all folks resist change.
He said, "It's as plain as the nose on your face,
there's nothing about it that's strange.

"In the first place, most people will feel very smug
in a job they have handled for years;
but change it around so they don't know the job,
and their security changes to fears.

"It's especially true if the person concerned
is doing his job with great vim,
and then you suggest a newfangled way,
he feels you have criticized him.

"Some suggestions are objectively studied,
and the persons affected will curse
that the change that is planned by some 'expert'
is a change, not for better but for worse."

So now when I think about changes,
I remember what the old wise man said,
that resistance to change is as normal
as having a heart and a head.

There are three keys to being successful
in making the changes we should,
we should learn them and use them sincerely,
so people accept change as good.

First, we must study the people,
in a word, we call it *Empathy*,
We must put ourselves in their places
to know what their feelings will be.

Then we must *Communicate* clearly
and tell them the "why" and the "when,"
we must give them the facts and the figures
and answer all questions for them.

The third key we call *Participation*,
we simply ask them to assist
to decide the best time or method,
and we find they no longer resist.

If overcoming resistance is your problem,
the keys that will solve it are these,
"Empathy," "Communication," and "Participation"
and changes will take place with ease.

Donald L. Kirkpatrick

CONCLUSION
16

Effective boards do not just happen. They are the result of hard work by board volunteers and staff. Sufficient time must be devoted to their development. The key to an effective and efficient voluntary organization is in it's board.

In this book, we hope we have blended art and science, remembering that art only without science becomes manipulation. Science without art becomes autocracy. In both cases, it is the client who suffers.

We have written this book based on the premise that people, if asked to do meaningful work for a believable cause in an understandable framework, will respond.

Harold J. Seymour said it best:

> But all in all, I would beg you to believe—as I do now and always have—that most people are very wonderful indeed, that they almost always wish to do the right thing, and that their ultimate performance, when boldly challenged and confidently led, is usually far better than we have any right to expect. Study them and treat them well, for you need them more than money.[1]

We do not claim that all we have written has worked for everybody; but everything we have written has worked in many places. We do not claim that our ideas are necessarily new. The past has been a good teacher. Our book is a blend of new and old ideas presented in new ways and with new applications.

We have asked a number of board volunteers why they began to do more for an organization. What were the factors that "turned them on"? One business executive said, "I serve on several boards. What you want is more of me for you and less for *them*. You will have to *earn* more."

In answering the question, "what turned them on," a pattern emerged. We found that most board volunteers described clearly definable stages. Obviously not all board volunteers go through all stages. However, a large enough number did to form what we call the Involvement/Contribution Ratio (exhibit 104).

Basically, the graph illustrates that a board volunteer's contributions to a voluntary organization will increase in direct proportion to his/her involvement. It suggests that this involvement goes through definable stages and relative time periods.

The perpendicular axis refers to contributions—not only in dollars, but in time, in attendance at meetings and, in willingness to contribute company facilities and equipment. The horizontal axis refers to the relative length of time it takes to reach each level. Please remember that this ratio is not a scientific measurement, but merely a tool to use in considering how board volunteers develop.

Level 1—Awareness

A prospective board volunteer may or may not be aware of the organization. If the prospect is aware, then he/she has an image. If the image is positive or neutral, the environment is conducive to affiliation. If the image is negative, chances are slim for affiliation.

Level 2—Affiliation

In the board membership process this corresponds to selection, recruitment, and orientation. If affiliation is done well, the stage has been set for a developing board volunteer. This is the new board volunteer's *first* impression and the most important. At this point a willingness to contribute is exhibited.

Level 3—Observation

This is the most critical level. At this point a new board volunteer makes a decision. By observing the organization in action, the new board volunteer will either find that the organization's practice has met the promise of recruitment and orientation or does not measure up. If the organization does not measure up, the new board volunteer is almost inevitably and irretrievably lost. They die on board or leave.

If the organization does measure up, the board volunteer moves to the next level.

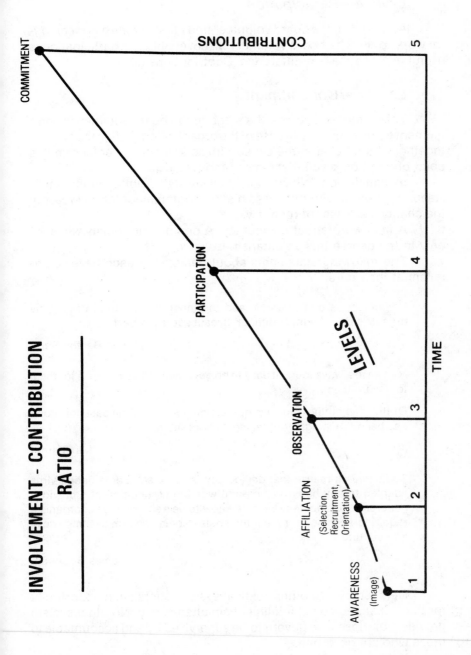

Exhibit 104

Level 4—Participation

At this level, the board volunteer finds that he/she has *meaningful* work to do. The board volunteer discovers his/her participation is useful and can make a difference. Contributions go up.

Level 5—Commitment

This is the final stage—the stage of the board volunteer's commitment to the cause or purpose of the organization. This is the coming together of the belief in the cause with solid management. From this point on the board volunteer is self-motivated.

In conclusion, please note that the fall *from* commitment is steep. If a board volunteer loses his/her commitment for any reason, the chances are slim of recovery.

A final word about democracy. A democratic society will exist only to the degree that voluntarism is viable.

The following statements about democracy each have voluntarism at their core:

Democracy is both the best and the most difficult form of political organization—the most difficult because it is the best.

Ralph Benton Perry

Men have always found it easy to be governed. What is hard is for them to govern themselves.

Of the many things we have done to democracy in the past, the worst has been the indignity of taking it for granted.

Max Lerner

Today we all realize that democracy is not a self-perpetuating virus adapted to any body politic—that was the assumption of a previous generation. Democracy we now know to be a special type of organism requiring specific nutriment materials—some economic, some social and cultural.

James B. Conant

Democracy! No other political system offers such opportunity for individual and social fulfillment simultaneously. No other system provides for those who govern to be supervised by and accountable to those who are governed.

Yet this system, which provides both for individual freedom and

the collective good, contains within itself the seeds of its own destruc-
tion. As more and more individuals attain success—in whatever form
they perceive success—subtle changes begin to erode the promise of a
democratic society. These changes give birth to two situations which
characterize sclerotic, moribund democracy:

—Unenlightened self-interest

—Selective democracy

Unenlightened self-interest is characterized by the rise of
materialism at the expense of intellectual and spiritual values. Self-
gratification at any cost dominates. "What's in it for me?" (at the expense of others) is the common attitude. There is a tendency to enjoy
what has been achieved. Motivation to action is primarily for "more"
and "better," regardless of side effects. Special-interest groups grow
stronger as individuals band together for greater leverage. Adversary
relationships replace collaboration. Yet the vast majority doze off in
front of the television set or survey society from the ostrich position.

Selective democracy is the result of a desire on the part of the
majority to consolidate and protect their gains. Prosperity comes at the
expense of others. Democracy becomes the means to deprive individuals or groups of their economic, educational, and political rights.
The very system that guarantees such rights philosophically is used
to withhold such rights operationally. While this book is not a definitive study of democracy, the authors have attempted to underline the
warnings of Messrs. Perry, Lerner, and Conant, as well as the following
caution from Saul Alinsky:

> There can be no democracy unless it is a dynamic democracy. When
> our people cease to participate—to have a place in the sun—then all of
> us will wither in the darkness of decadence. All of us will become mute,
> demoralized, lost souls.
>
> Rules for Radicals

These men are all saying something very significant. We must
work the system, not *replace* it. Although the ever-rising cry is to
abolish the system, the problems and evils of democracy are not in-
herent, and its deficiencies are found, not in the concept itself, but in
its practice. To make the system work, we must begin with *people*. And
people's attitudes are largely determined by the societal conditions in
which they find themselves. Gardner puts it this way:

> As a society (or institution) matures there is a subtle but pervasive
> shift in attitudes toward what is possible. The youthful attitude that

"anything is possible" is encountered less frequently, and there are more experts on why "it can't be done." The consequences are predictable: fewer mistakes—and less innovation. Confidence born of ignorance and inexperience is not so contemptible a quality as some imagine.

But of course life cannot be lived in utter disregard of the real limitations that surround performance. And in fact the appraisals which most people make of the limits of the possible are based on *some* solid evidence. The fatalism of the Asian peasant is not really surprising, in view of the evidence before him. Men will harbor a hopeful view of what man can achieve only if their societies do, in fact, offer some scope for individual accomplishment. If their societies provide them with the opportunity to grow as individuals and to have an impact on their environment, their attitudes will reflect those realities.[2]

All this has significance for our voluntary boards. The cry is heard ever more loudly that the board concept is an anachronism and should be drastically altered or abolished. This would be a tragic approach; for boards, with their concept of citizen involvement, are fundamental to democracy. True, they are complex and difficult to operate effectively. The rewards, however, are worth the effort.

For a board to be effective, special effort and understanding is required on the part of staff and board volunteers. If both are willing to work at the concept within the parameters outlined in this book, we will have successful boards, successful organizations, and a strengthened democracy. Our voluntary organizations will prosper. The eighteenth century German publicist, Friedrich von Goetz, offered this formula:

Two principles govern the moral and intellectual world. One is perpetual progress, the other is the necessary limitations to that progress. If the former alone prevailed, there would be nothing steadfast and durable on earth, and the whole social life would be the sport of winds and waves. If the latter had exclusive sway, or even if it obtained a mischievous preponderancy, everything would petrify or rot. The best ages of the world are those in which these two principles are the most equally balanced. In such ages every enlightened man ought to adopt both principles, and with one hand develop what he can; with the other, restrain and uphold what he ought.

NOTES

1. Seymour, *Designs for Fund-raising*, p. 16.
2. Gardner, *Self Renewal*.

THE BYLAWS

Appendix I

The articles of incorporation are those documents, filed with the state, upon which the not-for-profit status is granted. When was the last time these documents were pulled out of the safe for examination? There are organizations of many years' existence that have never examined their legal documents—or did so too long ago. In that interim, many things in the organization may have changed, and there should have been corresponding changes in the articles of incorporation. The point is, these documents should be examined on a periodic basis. Although legal problems rarely arise, the possibility is always there, and in order to avoid a legal challenge to your organization, you must check those articles of incorporation.

The bylaws are the documents through which the voluntary organization operates. If either staff member or board volunteer has a question about the organization, or about a function of the organizations, the bylaws are the final arbiter. They can be amended or changed only by action of the board of directors.

A word of caution to staff members: One of the easiest traps to fall into is to modify or change your organization in some way without first seeking the required action by the board of directors. The bylaws are your basic operating policies. Don't ignore or neglect them. Treat them with due respect.

Our model, the Newport Organization, has four units, each of which has a board of managers. Hence, there are board of managers' bylaws governing the operation of each unit.

The board of managers' bylaws are, in effect, the commissioning document of the board of directors. They are adaptable to any size organization. The following is a check-list of points which should be covered in the bylaws:

1. A statement of purpose
2. A description of the voting membership (board members)
3. Tenure of service
4. Number of meetings
5. Number and description of standing committees
6. Description and responsibilities of executive committee
7. Election of officers
8. Terms of officers
9. Appointment of committee chairperson
10. Tenure of chairperson
11. Annual meeting
12. Quorums
13. Filling of vacancies
14. Employment of staff
15. Amendments
16. Special meetings
17. Required reports
18. Removal of officers
19. Statement of fiscal year
20. Bank accounts, deposits, and disbursement of funds
21. Conflict of interest
22. Indemnification
23. Parliamentary authority

The following is a sample of Corporate bylaws:

BYLAWS
OF
NEWPORT ORGANIZATION

ARTICLE I

Purposes

The purposes of this corporation, as stated in its Articles of Incorporation, are exclusively charitable and educational and solely in furtherance thereof:

> The purposes of the corporation, as stated in its certificate of incorporation, are the education, guidance, physical well-being and training of boys and girls and, in furtherance thereof, the maintenance and operation of clubs, clubhouses, camps, farms, and other facilities and the conducting of classes, courses, and activities in connection therewith, without regard to race, creed, or national origin.

No part of the net earnings of the corporation shall inure to the benefit of any private individual, no part of the activities of the corporation shall be carrying on propaganda or otherwise attempting to influence legislation, and the corporation shall not participate in, or intervene in (including the publishing or distributing of statements) any political campaign on behalf of any candidate for public office.

Upon Dissolution of this corporation, all of its net assets shall be distributed to such charitable and educational organizations, as described in section 501 (c)(3) of the Internal Revenue Code of 1954, and similar sections of future laws, as the directors in their sole discretion shall determine.

ARTICLE II

The corporation shall maintain in the State a registered office and a registered agent at such office, and may have other offices within or without the state.

ARTICLE III

Board of Directors

3.1 GENERAL POWERS.   The affairs of the corporation shall be managed by its board of directors (Board).

3.2 NUMBER, TENURE AND QUALIFICATION.   The number of directors shall be not less than 7. Beginning at the organizational meeting held in 1978, one-third of the Board shall be elected for a term of one year, one-third for a term of two years and one-third for a term of three years and thereafter each director shall be elected for a term of three years and until successors shall have been elected. Directors shall be elected by directors at an annual meeting. Directors need not be residents.

3.3 REGULAR MEETINGS. A regular annual meeting of the Board shall be held each year without notice other then these bylaws, on the first Monday in March at the hour of 12:00 noon at the registered office of the corporation, or at such other time and place as the Board shall select. The Board shall provide by resolution for the holding of additional regular meetings which may be held without notice other than by such resolution. The Board shall meet at least once each calendar quarter.

3.4 SPECIAL MEETINGS. Special meetings of the Board may be called by the Chairperson or any two directors. The persons calling special meetings may fix the place for holding any special meeting called by them.

3.5 NOTICE. Written notice of any special meeting shall be given to each director at least forty-eight hours in advance at the director's address shown in the corporate records. If mailed, notice shall be deemed delivered when deposited in the United States mail, postage prepaid, in a sealed addressed envelope. Notice of any special meeting may be waived in writing signed either before or after the meeting by the persons entitled to notice. The attendance of a director at any meeting shall waive notice of such meeting, except where a director attends a meeting for the express purpose of objecting to the transaction of business because the meeting is not lawfully called. The business to be transacted at, or the purpose of, any regular or special meeting need not be specified in the notice or waiver of notice of such meeting, unless specifically required by law or by these bylaws. A meeting attended by all directors of the corporation shall be a valid meeting without notice.

3.6 QUORUM. One-third of the directors shall constitute a quorum for the transaction of business, provided that if less than one-third of the directors are present at any meeting, a majority of directors present may adjourn the meeting to another time without further notice.

3.7 MANNER OF ACTING. The act of a majority of directors present at a meeting at which a quorum is present shall be the act of the Board, unless the act of a greater number is required by statute, or by the bylaws.

3.8 INFORMAL ACTION BY DIRECTORS. Any action required to be taken, or which may be taken, at a meeting of directors, may be taken without a meeting if a written consent setting forth the action taken, is signed by all of the directors entitled to vote with respect to the action.

3.9 CONFLICT OF INTEREST. Any possible conflict of interest on the part of a director shall be disclosed to the Board. When any such interest becomes a matter of Board Action, such director shall not vote or use personal influence on the matter, and shall not be counted in the quorum for a meeting at which Board action is to be taken on the interest. The Director may, however, briefly state a position on the matter, and answer pertinent questions of Board members. The minutes of all actions taken on such matters shall clearly reflect that these requirements have been met.

3.10 VACANCIES. Any vacancy occurring in the Board or any directorship to be filled by reason of an increase in the number of directors shall be filled by the Board. A director elected to fill a vacancy shall be elected for the unexpired term of the director's predecessor in office.

3.11 COMPENSATION. Directors shall not receive any salaries for their services, but by resolution of the Board, expenses of attendance may be allowed for each regular or special meeting.

ARTICLE IV

Officers

4.1 OFFICERS. The officers of the corporation are Chairperson of the Board, vice chairperson—program, vice chairperson—resource development, vice chairperson and treasurer—business, vice chairperson—personnel, secretary, and such assistant treasurers, assistant secretaries or other officers as may be elected by the Board. Officers whose authority and duties are not prescribed in the bylaws shall have such authority and duties as prescribed by the Board. Any two or more offices may be held by the same person, except the offices of Chairperson and secretary.

4.2 ELECTION AND TERM OF OFFICE. The officers shall be elected annually by the Board at its annual meeting. The Chairperson, vice chairperson and secretary shall be elected from among members of the Board; the president shall not be a member of the Board.

4.3 REMOVAL. Any officer may be removed by the Board whenever in its judgment the best interests of the corporation would be served, but without prejudice to the contract rights, if any, of the officer.

4.4   CHAIRPERSON.   The Chairperson shall be the principal executive officer of the corporation. Subject to the direction and control of the Board, the Chairperson shall see that the resolutions and directives of the Board are carried into effect; and, in general, shall discharge all duties incident to the office of Chairperson and as prescribed by the Board. The Chairperson shall preside at all meetings of the Board. Except in those instances in which the authority to execute is expressly delegated to another officer or agent of the corporation, or a different mode of execution is expressly prescribed by the Board, the Chairperson may execute for the corporation any contracts, deeds, mortgages, bonds, or other instruments which the Board has authorized either individually or attested to by the secretary, an assistant secretary, or any other officer, according to the requirements of the instrument. The Chairperson may vote all securities which the corporation is entitled to vote except to the extent a different corporate officer or agent is authorized by the Board.

4.5   VICE CHAIRPERSON.   The vice chairperson shall assist the Chairperson in the discharge of the Chairperson's duties as the Chairperson may direct and shall perform such other duties as may be assigned by the Chairperson or by the Board. Vice Chairpersons are elected by the Board from a slate recommended by the Chairperson. In the event of absence, inability or refusal of the Chairperson to act, the vice chairperson in the order designated below, shall perform the duties of the Chairperson with all the power of, and subject to all the restrictions upon, the Chairperson.

4.6a   VICE CHAIRPERSON—PROGRAM.   The vice chairperson—program shall serve as chairperson of the Program Committee, and shall perform such other duties as may be assigned by the Chairperson or by the Board.

4.6b   VICE CHAIRPERSON—RESOURCE DEVELOPMENT. The vice chairperson—resource development shall serve as chairperson of the Resource Development Committee, and shall perform such other duties as may be assigned by the Chairperson or by the Board.

4.6c   VICE CHAIRPERSON AND TREASURER—BUSINESS. The vice chairperson and treasurer shall be the principal accounting and financial officer of the corporation and shall be responsible for the maintenance of adequate corporate books of account; have charge and custody of all corporate funds and securities, and be responsible for the receipt and disbursement thereof; shall serve as chairperson of the Business Committee; and perform all the duties incident to the office of treasurer and such other duties as may be assigned by the Chairperson or by the Board. If required by the Board, the treasurer shall give a bond for the faithful discharge of duties in such sum and form as the Board shall determine.

4.6d   VICE CHAIRPERSON—PERSONNEL.   The vice chairperson—personnel shall serve as chairperson of the Personnel Committee, and shall perform such other duties as may be assigned by the Chairperson or by the Board.

4.7   SECRETARY.   The secretary shall record the minutes of the meetings of the Board; see that notices are given in accordance with the bylaws or as required by law; keep the corporate records and seal; keep a register of the address furnished to the secretary by each member; and perform all duties incident to the office of secretary and such other duties as may be assigned by the Chairperson or by the Board.

4.8   ASSISTANT TREASURERS AND ASSISTANT SECRETARIES.   The assistant treasurers and assistant secretaries shall perform such duties as shall be assigned to them by the treasurer or the secretary, respectively, or by the Chairperson or the Board. If required by the Board, the assistant treasurers shall give bond for the faithful discharge of their duties in such sum and form as the Board shall determine.

ARTICLE V

Employed Staff

5.1   EXECUTIVE DIRECTOR.   The Board shall employ an Executive Director who shall be the chief operational officer of the corporation. Subject to the Board, the Executive Director shall have general direction over the operations of the corporation; shall implement all policies of the Board; shall submit to the Board or its committees such reports as the Board may require; shall assist in the preparation of an annual budget for presentation to and adoption by the Board; shall assist in the preparation of a personnel policy; provide staff support to the Board; and shall perform such other functions as the Board may direct. The Executive Director shall be responsible directly to the

Board of Directors and shall attend all meetings of the Board and its committees without vote.

5.2   OTHER STAFF.   Such employed staff as may be necessary to support the organization shall be hired and discharged by the Executive Director. The employed staff shall report directly to, and are accountable to, the Executive Director or his or her designates.

ARTICLE VI

Committees

6.1   COORDINATING COMMITTEE.   The Coordinating Committee shall consist of the Chairperson, the Vice Chairperson, Secretary, and two Directors elected annually by the Board. The responsibility of the Coordinating Committee is to direct the planning function. It has no authority to act in the name of the Board of Directors.

6.2   STANDING COMMITTEES.   The corporation shall have the following standing committees which shall be advisory to the Board: Program Committee, Resource Development Committee, Business Committee, and Personnel Committee. Members of standing committees shall be appointed by the Board. A majority of members of each standing committee shall be directors. The duties of the standing committees shall be adopted by the Board.

6.3   OTHER COMMITTEES.   Other committees not exercising the authority of the Board may be designated by a resolution adopted by a majority of directors present at a meeting at which a quorum is present. Except as otherwise provided in such resolution, the Chairperson of the corporation shall appoint and remove committee members whenever the best interests of the corporation are served thereby.

6.4   TERM OF OFFICE.   Each committee member shall serve until the next annual meeting of the corporation and until a successor is appointed, unless the member is removed from, or ceases to qualify as, a member of the committee, or unless the committee is sooner terminated.

6.5   VACANCIES.   Vacancies in the membership of any committee may be filled by appointments made in the same manner as in the case of the original appointments.

6.6   QUORUM.   Unless otherwise provided in the resolution

designating a committee, a majority of the committee shall constitute a quorum and the act of a majority of the members present at a meeting at which a quorum is present shall be the act of the committee.

6.7 RULES.   Each committee may adopt governing rules not inconsistent with these bylaws or with rules adopted by the Board.

ARTICLE VII

Indemnification

7.1 ACTION BY OTHER THAN CORPORATION. The corporation shall indemnify any person who was or is a party or is threatened to be made a party to any threatened, pending, or completed action, suit or proceeding, whether civil, criminal, administrative or investigative (other than an action by or in the right of the corporation) by reason of the fact that such person is or was a director, or officer of the corporation, or is or was serving at the request of the corporation as a director or officer, of another corporation, partnership, joint venture, trust or other enterprise, against expenses (including attorneys' fees), judgments, fines and amounts paid in settlement actually and reasonably incurred by such person in connection with such action, suit or proceeding if such person acted in good faith and in a manner which such person reasonably believed to be in or not opposed to the best interests of the corporation, and, with respect to any criminal action or proceeding, had no reasonable cause to believe the conduct was unlawful. The termination of any action, suit or proceeding by judgment, order, settlement, conviction, or upon a plea of nolo contendere or its equivalent, shall not, of itself, create a presumption that the person did not act in good faith and in a manner which the person reasonably believed to be in or not opposed to the best interests of the corporation, and, with respect to any criminal action or proceeding, had reasonable cause to believe that the person's conduct was unlawful.

7.2 ACTION BY CORPORATION. The corporation shall indemnify any person who was or is a party or is threatened to be made a party to any threatened, pending or completed action or suit by or in the right of the corporation to procure a judgment in its favor by reason of the fact that such person is or was a director or officer, of the corporation, or is or was serving at the request of the corporation as a director or officer of another corporation, partnership, joint venture, trust or other enterprise against expenses (including attorneys' fees) actually and reasonably believed to be in or not opposed to the best interests of the corporation and except that no indemnification shall be made in respect of any claim, issue or matter as to which such person shall have been adjudged to be liable for willful negligence or misconduct in the performance of duty to the corporation unless and only to the extent that the court in which such action or suit was brought shall determine upon application that, despite the adjudication of liability but in view of all the circumstances of the case, such person is fairly and reasonably entitled to indemnity for such expenses which the court shall deem proper.

7.3 EXPENSES. To the extent that a director or officer has been successful on the merits or otherwise in defense of any action, suit or proceeding referred to in Sections 1 and 2 above, or in defense of any claim, issue or matter therein, such director or officer shall be indemnified against expenses (including attorneys' fees) actually and reasonably incurred in connection therewith.

7.4 PREREQUISITES. Any indemnification under Sections 1 and 2 above (unless ordered by a court) shall be made by the corporation only as authorized in the specific case upon a determination that indemnification of the director or officer is proper in the circumstances because the director or officer has met the applicable standard of conduct set forth in Sections 1 and 2. Such determination shall be made (1) by the Board by a majority vote of a quorum consisting of directors who were not parties to such action, suit or proceeding, or (2) if such a quorum is not obtainable, or, even if obtainable a quorum of disinterested directors so directs, by independent legal counsel in a written action.

7.5 ADVANCES BY CORPORATION. Expenses incurred in defending a civil or criminal action, suit cr proceeding may be paid by the corporation in advance of the final disposition of such action, suit or proceeding as authorized by the Board in the specific case upon receipt of an undertaking by or on behalf of the director or officer, to repay such amount unless it shall ultimately be determined that the director or officer is entitled to be indemnified by the corporation as authorized in this article.

7.6 OTHER REMEDIES. The indemnification provided by this article shall not be deemed exclusive of any other rights to which such director or officer may be entitled under any agreement, vote of disinterested directors or otherwise, both as to action in any official capacity and as to action in another capacity while holding such office, and shall continue as to a person who has ceased to be a director or officer, and shall inure to the benefit of the heirs, executors and administrators of such a person.

7.7 INSURANCE. The corporation may purchase and maintain insurance on behalf of any person who may be indemnified here against any liability asserted against such person and incurred in any capacity, or arising out of any status, for which the person may be indemnified.

ARTICLE VIII

Miscellaneous

8.1 CONTRACTS. The Board may authorize any officer or agent of the corporation, in addition to the officers authorized by the bylaws, to enter into any contract or execute and deliver any instrument in the name of, and on behalf of, the corporation. Such authority may be general or confined to specific instances.

8.2 CHECKS, DRAFTS, ETC. All orders for the payment of money, or evidences of indebtedness issued in the name of the corporation, shall be signed by such corporate officer or agent as the Board shall determine. In the absence of such a determination, such instruments shall be signed by the treasurer or an assistant treasurer and countersigned by the Chairperson or a vice chairperson.

8.3 DEPOSITS. All corporate funds shall be deposited to the credit of the corporation in such banks, or other depositaries as the Board may select.

8.4 GIFTS. The Board may accept on behalf of the corporation any contribution, gift, bequest or devise for the general, or for any special, corporate purpose.

8.5 RECORDS. The corporation shall keep, at the registered or principal office, complete books of account, minutes of the proceedings of directors and committees having any authority of the Board, and a record with the names and addresses of directors. All corporate records may be inspected by any director, or the director's agent or attorney for any proper purpose at any reasonable time.

8.6 FISCAL YEAR. The fiscal year of the corporation shall end on December 31 of each year.

8.7 SEAL. The corporate seal shall have inscribed on it the name of the corporation and the words "Corporate Seal, Illinois."

8.8 WAIVER OF NOTICE. Whenever any notice is required to be given, a waiver in writing signed by the persons entitled to such notice, whether before or after the time stated therein, shall be deemed equivalent to the giving of notice.

ARTICLE IX

Amendments

The bylaws may be altered, amended, or repealed or new bylaws adopted by affirmative vote of a majority of the Board. Such action may be taken at any regular or special meeting of the Board for which notice of the proposed action shall have been given in accordance with the bylaws.

ARTICLE X

Parliamentary Authority

The rules contained in Robert's Rules of Order, Newly Revised, shall govern the Newport Organization in all cases wherein they are not superseded by the bylaws or special rules of order.

If your organization is, like the Newport Organization, multi-unit, the following Article should be included in your corporate bylaws.

ARTICLE XI

Operation of Units

The Board of Managers of each Unit is established by the Board of Directors and shall at all times be subject to the direction of the President of the Corporation. The Unit Director shall at all times be subject to the direction of the President of the Corporation through the Executive Director.

The Board of Managers shall be responsible for the management of the affairs of such Units, subject to the limitation of these bylaws and the Board of Managers bylaws. All action of the Board of Managers shall be subject to the approval of the Board of Directors, shall meet no less than six (6) times annually, and the annual business meeting shall be in November of each year. The nominee for the Chairmanship of the Board of Managers shall be presented to the Nominating Committee of the Board of Directors. The Chairman of the Board of Managers shall be a member of the Board of Directors and shall serve on the Board of Directors during his term of office as such Chairman. He shall also serve on the Executive Committee. Such Board of Managers, insofar as may be feasible, shall be constituted of persons living or conducting business establishments in or about the neighborhood of such Unit. The Board of Managers shall be evaluated annually. The rules and bylaws pertaining to the management and operation of each Unit shall be such as may be prescribed from time to time by the Board of Directors of the Corporation. The Board of Directors of the Corporation may likewise appoint, or authorize the President of the Corporation to appoint, such other persons as may be necessary to operate and supervise any such Unit.

Some multi-unit organizations have bylaws for the Units in addition to the above Article in the corporate bylaws. The following is a sample of unit bylaws.

Note: Unless they are also on the Board of Directors, members of the Board of Managers do not incur legal liability.

NEWPORT ORGANIZATION
BOARD OF MANAGERS
BYLAWS

*   *   *   *   *

ARTICLE I

Name

The name of the Unit shall be the _____Unit.

ARTICLE II

Object

The Unit shall be operated as a unit in furtherance of the purposes of the Newport Organization, a corporation organized and existing under the General Not-for-Profit Corporation Act of the State of

_____.

ARTICLE III

Board of Managers

Section 1. General Powers. A Board of Managers, to be

elected in the manner hereinafter set forth, shall act in a management capacity with respect to the operation of the Unit, and shall have such other and further duties and powers as may be specifically delegated to them from time to time by the Board of Directors of the Newport Organization, all of which duties and power shall at all times be subject to control and approval by the Directors of the NEWPORT ORGANIZATION. All voting rights shall be vested solely in such Board.

Section 2. Number. The number of Managers shall be not less than 25 and not more than 60, which number shall be approved by the Board of Directors.

Section 3. Qualifications. Insofar as may be feasible, the Board of Managers shall consist of persons residing or maintaining business addresses in the community in the neighborhood of the Unit. One-fifth (1/5) of the total Board of Managers membership must be neighborhood people, neighborhood people meaning residents in the general vicinity of the Unit.

Section 4. Initial Board of Managers. The initial Board of Managers constituted under these bylaws will be formed under the leadership of a Chairman of the Board of Managers appointed by the President of the Newport Organization. The Board of Managers shall be considered to be established after nine additional candidates have been approved by the Executive Committee. The Board of Managers shall be classified in respect of the time for which they shall severally hold office by dividing them into three classes, each class consisting of one-third (1/3) of the whole number of the Board of Directors.

The Managers of the first class shall be elected for a term of one year; the Managers of the second class shall be elected for a term of two years; and the Managers of the third class shall be elected for a term of three years. At each November meeting, the successors to the Managers of the class whose term shall expire in that year, shall be elected by the Board of Managers to hold office for the term of three years so that the term of office of one class of Managers shall expire in each year.

In case of any increase in the number of Managers, the additional Managers shall be elected by the Managers then in office; one-third of such additional Managers for the unexpired portion of the term of two years, and one-third for the unexpired portion for the term of three years, so that each class of Managers shall be increased equally.

Each Manager shall hold office for the term for which he has been elected and until his successor shall have been elected.

In addition thereto, the Board, at any meeting called for that purpose, shall elect Managers to fill the vacancies created by the death, ineligibility or resignation of any Manager. Any Manager so elected to fill a vacancy shall hold office for the unexpired term of his predecessor and until his successor shall have been elected. If the election of Managers is not held at said November meeting, it may be held at any adjournment thereof or at any regular meeting or special meeting called for that purpose. If such election shall be held at any meeting other than the November meeting, a notice of such meeting, stating that such election will be held, shall be mailed to each member of the Board of Managers in accordance with Section 8 of this Article. The term Manager as herein used shall refer to a member of the Board of Managers.

Section 5. Annual Meetings. An annual meeting of the Board of Managers shall be held during January of the calendar year for the purpose of ceremonially inducting Managers and Officers and for the transaction of such other business as may come before the meeting. Such meeting shall be held at such place as the Managers shall designate, and if no such designation is made, then such meeting shall be held at the headquarters of the Unit.

Section 6. Regular Meetings. The Board of Managers shall regularly meet on such dates and times as designated by the Board of Managers. There shall be no less than six regularly scheduled Board of Managers meetings.

Section 7. Special Meetings. Special meetings of the Board of Managers may be called by the chairman and shall be called by him on the written request of not less than 5 Managers. Such request shall contain a summary of the proposals or business intended to be brought before the meeting. Any special meeting may be held at such place within the City of _____ as the chairman may determine.

Section 8. Notice. Notice of any special meeting of the Board of Managers shall be given at least three days previously thereto by written notice delivered personally or sent by mail or telegram to each Manager at his address as shown by the records of the Board of Managers. If mailed, such notice shall be deemed to be delivered when deposited in the United States mail in a sealed envelope so addressed with postage thereon prepaid. If notice be given by telegram such notice shall be deemed to be delivered when the telegram is delivered to the telegraph company. Any Manager may waive notice of any meetings. The attendance of a Manager at any meeting shall constitute a waiver of notice of such meeting, except where a Manager attends a meeting for the express purpose of objecting to the transaction of any business because the meeting is not lawfully called or convened. Neither the business to be transacted at, nor the purpose of, any regular or special meeting of the Board need be specified in the notice or waiver of notice of such meeting unless specifically required by law or by the bylaws.

Section 9.   Quorum.   One-third of whole Board of Managers shall constitute a quorum for the transaction of business at any meeting of the Board of Managers, provided that if a quorum shall not be present, the presiding officer shall adjourn the meeting from time to time without further notice.

Section 10.   Manner of Acting.   The act of a majority of the Board of Managers present at a meeting at which a quorum is present shall be the act of the Board of Managers.

ARTICLE IV

Officers

Section 1.   Number and Title.   The officers of the Unit shall be a chairman of the Board, one or more vice-chairmen of the Board (the number thereof to be determined by the Board of Managers), a secretary, a treasurer, and such other officers as may be elected in accordance with the provisions of this Article. The Board of Managers may elect or appoint such other officers as it shall deem necessary, shall sign such correspondence or other papers as may be assigned to him for attention or as shall require his signature as secretary.

He shall keep a register of the post office address of each Manager and Officer of the Unit and in general shall perform all duties incident to the office of secretary and such other duties as may from time to time be assigned to him by the chairman or the Board of Managers.

Section 2.   In addition to the foregoing officers to be elected by the Board of Managers, a Unit Director, a Director of Camps in the case of the camps, shall be employed by the Executive Director of the Newport Organization in consultation with the Board of Managers on an annual basis for such compensation as shall be fixed by the Board of Directors of the Newport Organization following consultation with the Chairman of the Board of Managers. The Executive Director shall have the authority to terminate a Unit Director or Director of Camps if necessary following consultation with the Chairman of the Board of

Managers. The Unit Director shall have general direction of the operation of the Unit and shall represent it in its relations with all other agencies and subject, however, to the general supervision of the Executive Director of the Newport Organization. He shall compile and submit to the Executive Director such reports, analyses, statistics, plans, and other information as may be required of him from time to time. His performance will be evaluated annually by the Executive Director and reviewed with the Personnel Committee of the Board of Managers. He shall be an ex-officio member of all standing committees and of the Board of Managers.

ARTICLE V

Section 1.   Standing Committees.   The following shall be the Standing Committees of the Unit:

Program Services and Personnel Committee
Resource Development Committee
Business Committee

In addition there shall be an Executive Committee.

The members and Chairman of each of the said committees and all such other committees as may be designated by the Board of Managers shall be members of the Board of Managers and shall be appointed by the Chairman, subject to the approval of the Managers. The Chairman of each Standing Committee shall be a member of the Board of Managers, shall be a member of the Executive Committee where feasible, and shall be appointed in December by the incoming Chairman. Each committee shall operate under guidelines provided for such committee by the Board of Managers.

(a)   Executive Committee shall consist of not less than seven (7) members, all of whom shall be members of the Board of Managers.

Meetings of such Committee may be held at the call of the Chairman of the Board of Managers or the Chairman of the Committee in the interim between meetings of the Board of Managers to consider and act upon emergency matters provided however that the authority herein conferred upon said committee shall not operate to relieve the Board of Managers or any individual Manager of any responsibility imposed upon it or him under these bylaws.

(b)   The Program Services and Personnel Committee shall consist of seven (7) or more members who shall be responsible for the planning, review and approval of both short-and long-range program services, and the supervision and evaluation of the various programs and activities in consort with the purpose of the Corporation. It should have as many Sub-Committees as is necessary to accomplish its commission. They could include: Education, Physical Activities, Recruitment and Training, Alumni and Membership, Health and Clinics, Vocational Training and Special Projects.

(c)   The Resource Development Committee shall consist of seven (7) or more members and shall be responsible for conducting an annual campaign, a program for recruitment and training of Board Members and a Public Relations program. It shall have as its subcommittees Campaign, Board Membership, and Public Relations.

(d)   The Business Committee shall consist of seven (7) members, including the treasurer of the Unit. It shall, in collaboration with the Development Committee, Program Services Committee and the Unit Director, recommend to the Board of Managers a yearly budget to be approved by the Board of Directors of the Newport Organizations. Special projects involving capital funds may be undertaken only if approved by the Board of Directors of the Newport Organization. Special endowment funds may be established only if approved by the Board of Directors of the Newport Organization. Recommendations on financial policy and planning may be made to the Finance Committee of the Newport Organization. It shall have as a sub-committee: Property.

(e)   A Board of Managers may have any number of sub- or ad-hoc committees, but no more than the number and title of Standing Committees noted in Article V, Section 1.

Section 2.   Nominating Committee.   The Nominating Committee shall consist of seven (7) or more members who shall be members of the Board of Managers and shall be elected no later than 60 days prior to the November business meeting.

The Nominating Committee shall prepare a single slate of candidates for all offices, members of the entire Board of Managers whose terms are expiring subject to and in conformity with Article IV, Section II, and file such slate in the office of the Unit Director no later than 30 days prior to the date of the November business meeting. The Unit Director shall mail a copy of said slate to all officers and Managers within 5 days after receiving same.

Section 3.   Term of Office.   Each member of a committee shall continue as such until December 31 and until his successor is appointed, unless the committee shall be sooner terminated, or unless members be removed from such committee, or unless such members shall cease to qualify as a member thereof. Vacancies in the membership of any committee may be filled by appointment made in the same manner as provided in the case of the original appointment.

Section 4.   Quorum.   A majority of the whole committee shall constitute a quorum, and the act of a majority of the members present at a meeting at which a quorum is present shall be the act of the Committee.

Section 5.   Rules.   Each committee may adopt rules for its own government not inconsistent herewith.

Section 6.   Reports.   Not later than the first day of_____ each year the chairman of each committee shall submit to the Board of Managers and to the Unit Director a written report of the activities of such committee during the preceding fiscal year. The Board of Managers shall comply with the guidelines of the Board of Directors of the Newport Organization.

ARTICLE VI

Membership In Unit

The members of the Unit shall consist of such boys and girls between the ages of 6 and 18, inclusive, as shall make application for membership in the Unit, and shall have completed such probationary period as the Unit Director shall deem necessary. Any such boy or girl who shall desire to use the facilities of the Unit after reaching the age of 19 may continue as an associate member of the Unit until he or she shall have reached the age of 21 years.

ARTICLE VII

Relationship Of Unit To Newport Organization

The Newport Organization through the Board of Directors shall have general authority and supervision over the Board of Managers. The Newport Organization through the Executive Director shall have general authority and supervision over the Unit and the Unit Directors. The Board of Managers shall advise with the Newport Organization on matters of local interest in the neighborhood served by the Unit and the needs of the Unit and shall provide the Board of Directors with the minutes of the Unit Board of Managers. In January of each year the chairpersons of each of the Unit standing committees will meet under the chairmanship of the corresponding corporate standing committees.

ARTICLE VIII
Authority To Incur Expenditures
Or Liabilities

No Manager, officer, or other representative of the Unit shall authorize or make any expenditure or commit the Unit or Newport Organization to any liability whatsoever, unless such expenditure or liability shall have been previously approved by the Newport Organization, or set up in a budget approved by such corporation. [*VERY IMPORTANT!*]

ARTICLE IX
Fiscal Year

The fiscal year of the Unit shall begin on the first day of January and end on the last day of December in each year.

ARTICLE X
Amendments To Bylaws

These bylaws may be altered, amended or repealed, and new bylaws may be adopted by a majority of the Board of Managers present at any regular meeting or at any special meeting provided (1) that at least 5 days written notice is given of intention to alter, amend or repeal or to adopt new bylaws at such meeting, and (2) that any proposed change in the bylaws of the Unit shall have been previously approved by the Board of Directors of the Newport Organization.

THE COMMITTEE COMMISSION

Appendix II

A voluntary organization is dependent upon a board and committee structure with well-defined responsibilities on all levels.

Just as a professional staff person must have a job description, each committee must have a commission which spells out what functions are expected. Thus, each person in the organization sees clearly where he or she fits in the total scheme of things.

Following are sample commissions for standing committees and sub-committees.

      *   *   *   *   *

TO: The Executive Committee

FROM: The Board of Directors

General Commission

The Executive Committee is commissioned by and responsible to the Board of Directors of the Newport Organization to function on behalf of the Board of Directors in matters of emergency and in interim periods between regularly scheduled Board meetings. The Executive Committee shall have and exercise the authority of the Board of Directors provided that such authority shall not operate to circumvent the responsibility and authority vested in the Board of Directors by the Newport Organization's Bylaws.

Appointments and Composition

    1.   The Executive Committee shall be composed of the officers

of the Board of Directors and the Chairmen of all standing committees.

2. The Chairmen of the Unit Boards of Managers are members of the Executive Committee for the duration of their office.

3. Chairmen of ad-hoc committees may be appointed by the Board Chairman for the duration of the committee function.

4. Immediate past officers of the Board may be appointed to the Executive Committee at the discretion of the Board Chairman.

5. The Executive Director is ex-officio member of the Executive Committee.

Responsibilities

1. *To respond* to the call of the Board Chairman or Executive Director for emergency meetings to deal with special problems between regular Board meetings.

2. *Meet* during those months when no regular Board meetings are held to deal with on-going, organizational concerns.

3. *Review* quarterly all committee reports to assure relevant Board meeting agenda and to bring to the attention of the Board any problems which might otherwise escape action.

*   *   *   *   *

TO: The Finance Committee

FROM: The Board of Directors

General Commission

The Finance Committee is commissioned by and responsible to the Board of Directors of the Newport Organization to assume the primary relationship in matters pertaining to the Newport Organization's purposes, maintain quality programs and services and perform the following functions subject to and in conformity with established policies of the Newport Organization and the approval of the Board of Directors.

Appointments and Composition

1. Appointments to the Finance Committee are made in

December of each year by the Chairperson of the Unit Board of Managers for the following fiscal year.

2. The Finance Committee shall include a chairperson, the treasurer of the Board of Directors and a minimum of three other Board of Director members.

3. Additional members may be appointed from the Board of Directors as needed and according to particular ability.

Responsibilities

1. *Appoint* and supervise the Investment Committee which has the responsibility for the endowment and investment portfolios.

2. *Appoint* and supervise the Property Committee which has responsibility for the physical facilities.

3. *Participate* in the preparation of the organization's budget as outlined in the Corporate Budgeting Process.

4. *Review* monthly finance reports received from accounting and report to the Board of Directors on the financial operation.

5. *Control* current financial operations within the limit of the total approved budget.

6. *Prepare* for the Board of Directors' meeting at the beginning of each calendar quarter a financial projection for the current year and make appropriate recommendations concerning necessary actions to achieve a balanced budget.

7. *Organize* and establish such sub-committees as may be required to further its work and fulfill its functions.

*   *   *   *   *

TO: The Resource Development Committee

FROM: The Board of Directors

General Commission

The Resource Development Committee is commissioned by and responsible to the Board of Directors of the Newport Organization to assume the primary relationship in matters pertaining to campaign, public relations, planned giving, capital giving, and board membership in accordance with the established policies and practices approved by the Board of Directors of the Newport Organization.

Appointments and Composition

1. The Chairperson of the Resource Development Committee is appointed by the Chairperson of the Board of Managers.

2. The Resource Development Committee is composed of the Chairperson and Vice Chairperson of the Resource Development Committee and the chairperson of the sub-committees on campaign, board membership, public relations, planned giving, capital giving. Other members can be appointed as deemed necessary.

Responsibilities

1. *Supervise* the functions of its sub-committees.

2. *Participate* in the budget process of the organization as outlined in that process.

3. *Maintain* open communication with the Resource Development Committees of the Units.

4. *Conduct* at least two orientation and planning meetings with the Resource Development Committees of the Units.

5. *Meet* regularly with the chairpersons of the Unit Resource Development Committees.

6. *Ensure* that the corporate and unit sub-committees of the respective resource development committees meet on a regular basis.

*   *   *   *   *

COMMISSION FOR A CORPORATE BOARD
PERSONNEL COMMITTEE

TO: The Personnel Committee

FROM: The Board of Directors

General Commission

The Personnel Committee is commissioned by, and responsible to, the Board of Directors of the Newport Organization to assume the responsibility for advising it on matters pertaining to Personnel Administration and staffing of the Units, so that all functions of the organization may be effectively and efficiently carried forth in conformity with the established policies and practices approved by the Board of Directors of the Newport Organization.

Appointments and Composition

1. Appointments to the Personnel Committee are made on an annual basis by the Chairperson of the Board of Directors for the ensuing year.

2. The Personnel Committee shall have sixteen (16) members. The Personnel Committee may include members not on the Board of Directors.

Responsibilities

1. *Provide* overall policy guidance for personnel operations in the Newport Organization.

2. *Submit*, for final approval, recommendations on Personnel policy matters to the Executive Committee of the Board of Directors.

3. *Provide* general supervision of personnel operations in the areas of:

   a. Policy revision

   b. Salary administration

   c. Fringe benefits administration

   d. Staff development and training

   e. Recruitment and retention

   f. Employee relations

4. *Review*, with the Executive Director, the staffing design of the Unit for the coming year.

5. The Chairperson of the Personnel Committee serves, with other committee chairmen, on an Ad-Hoc Budget Committee to recommend salaries.

6. *Review* staff additions and terminations and make periodic reports to the Board of Directors on the general state of

staff capability for the meeting of the Newport Organization's objectives.

*   *   *   *   *

COMMISSION FOR A CORPORATE BOARD PROGRAM SERVICES COMMITTEE

TO: Program Services Committee

FROM: Board of Directors

General Commission

The Program Services Committee has the primary responsibility for the overall program emphasis of the Newport Organization. It shall develop programs and monitor program goals with the involvement of the total organization.

Appointments and Composition

1. Appointments to the Program Services Committee will be made by the Chairperson of the Board of Directors on an annual basis with the advice and consent of the Chairperson of the Program Services Committee for the ensuing year.

2. The Committee shall consist of sixteen (16) members, including the Chairperson of the Unit Program Services and Personnel Committee.

3. Any number of sub-committees may be appointed, and non-board members may be appointed to serve.

Responsibilities

1. *Meet* the fourth Tuesday in the months of March, June, September, and December.

2. *Develop* program services action goals, both long and short term.

3. *Plan and develop* program services and monitor the progress toward the stated objectives.

4. *Evaluate* shifts in program services with emphasis on the necessary recommendations for policy changes.

5. *Evaluate* services.

6. *Appraise* jointly with the Resource Development Committee

those increases and decreases which involve financing, for suitable recommendations to the Executive Committee.

7. *Support and enhance* the existing program of the Newport Organization by bringing to it new resources and ideas. (This can be accomplished by Program Services Committee members' serving on the sub-committees of the Newport Organization.)

8. *Evaluate and recommend* new programs to the Board in line with the purpose and objectives of the Newport Organization. (This function will be carried out by the Program Services Committee as new major programs are recommended by professional staff or lay boards. The Program Services Committee evaluates the suggested new programs and makes its recommendations to the Executive Committee of the Board of Directors.)

9. *Interpret* the Program Services of the Newport Organization to the Board of Directors of the Newport Organization in order that members of the Board are aware of, and understand, these services. This could be accomplished by means of the following:

   a. Special tours of Units and camps by the Board, sponsored by the Program Services Committee.

   b. Special program presentations in Board meetings.

   c. Special printed materials, which the Board would receive from time to time, informing them of current program services.

*   *   *   *   *

COMMISSION FOR A UNIT PROGRAM SERVICES AND
PERSONNEL COMMITTEE

TO: The Program Services and Personnel Committee

FROM: The Board of Managers

General Commission

The Program Services and Personnel Committee is responsible to the Board of Managers of Unit One of the Newport Organization and is commissioned by them to assume the primary responsibility for all program concerns and activities sponsored by, or taking place in, Unit

One. This committee is also responsible for seeing that all such activity is in accord with the purposes, policies, and practices approved by the Board of Directors of the Newport Organization.

Appointments and Composition

1. The Chairman of the Program Services and Personnel Committee is appointed by the Chairman of the Unit Board of Managers for the ensuing year.

2. Said Committee shall include all chairpersons of standing program sub-committees. These sub-committee chairmen are appointed by the Program Services and Personnel Committee Chairman in consultation with the Board Chairman, the Unit Director, and the Unit Program Director.

3. Other members may be appointed from the directorate, or from the community at large, in accordance with their particular capabilities in specialized fields.

4. The Program Services and Personnel Committee shall include older youth and community representatives.

Responsibilities

1. *Formulate* a written policy governing all phases of program and services provided by the Unit, subject to the approval of the Board of Managers. This policy is a composite of the Policy statements of the various program sub-committees. Review this policy annually to ensure that practice is in step with changing needs.

2. *Assume* responsibility for initiating the establishment of such sub-committees as are necessary to provide a well-rounded program within the Unit.

3. *Determine* the constituency (make-up of the groups to be served) in accordance with Unit policy.

4. *Initiate and authorize* the establishment of such program services or events as are necessary or desirable to carry out the purposes of the Unit and the needs of the community.

5. *Establish* with the Program Director priorities for program emphasis in use of staff time and building space.

6. *Provide* counsel to the Program Director in the management and activities of his department.

7. *Aid* in the recruitment of voluntary leadership.

8. *Study and evaluate* purpose, procedures, and results of program activity.

9. *Maintain records* of participation in all program services and events according to procedure and policy.

10. *Study* youth constituency in terms of age, sex, and groups served, and make recommendations on how to serve better a larger number.

11. *Submit* a written monthly program report to the Board of Managers.

12. *Submit* to the Finance Committee in _____ of each year a proposed budget for the operation of the Program Department. This is a composite of the budget of all program sub-committees. It should include anticipated cost of part-time personnel, equipment, program expense, and so forth, as well as expected earned income.

13. *Awareness and effort* should be constant in terms of ways and means of increasing earned program income.

14. *Review*, with the Unit Director, the staffing design of the club for the coming year.

15. *Review* staff additions and terminations and make periodic reports to the Board of Managers on the general state of staff capability for meeting of the Unit's objectives.

(Note: The Program Services and Personnel Committee lends itself to a number of sub-committees. The possibilities depend upon the nature of the services delivered by the voluntary organization, but one example would be a physical activities sub-committee to serve as a youth agency.

As mentioned earlier, committees offer a fine opportunity to involve people in the operation of a voluntary organization without expanding and diluting the Board, and the program services area is fertile territory for this sort of involvement.)

*   *   *   *   *

COMMISSION FOR A PROPERTY SUB-COMMITTEE OF THE UNIT FINANCE COMMITTEE

TO: The Property Sub-Committee of the Finance Committee

FROM: The Finance Committee

General Commission

The Property Sub-Committee is commissioned by and responsible to the Finance Committee of Unit One of the Newport Organization to assume the primary relationship to matters pertaining to building care and maintenance, protecting the capital investment of the Newport Organization in buildings and grounds, and assuring the functional utility of all areas and equipment.

Appointments and Composition

1. Appointments to the Property Sub-Committee are made on an annual basis by the Chairperson of the Board of Managers and the Chairperson of the Finance Committee for the ensuing year.

2. The Chairperson of this Sub-Committee is to be a member of the Finance Committee.

3. Other members may be appointed from the community in accordance with particular capacities in specialized fields.

4. These members will be appointed by the Board Chairman and the Finance Committee Chairman upon recommendation of the Property Sub-Committee Chairman.

Responsibilities

1. *Make a complete inspection and evaluation* of building condition, noting all maintenance and repair needs of the Unit, in April of each year.

2. *Develop* a schedule for the completion of all needed heavy maintenance during the summer months.

3. *Develop* a schedule for routine and preventive maintenance, e.g., painting, boiler and equipment care.

4. *Make a monthly inspection* of the building and meet with the Unit Director for purposes of consultation and making suggestions relative to performance of maintenance staff.

5. *Appoint* one member of the Sub-Committee who will give regular attention to housekeeping, safety, and sanitation aspects of the building, and maintain communication with the Unit Director.

6. *Make brief written monthly reports* for the Board of Managers.

7. *Scrutinize* gas, electric, chemical, and cleaning-supply consumption in relation to budget and areas of possible waste.

8. *Prepare*, by May of each year, an estimated budget of spending necessary within this department, for study and incorporation into the Unit budget.

9. *Anticipate* any major maintenance problems for which special financing may be necessary, and notify the Finance Committee so that provisions can be made. Provide estimated costs with this report.

*   *   *   *   *

COMMISSION FOR A BOARD MEMBERSHIP SUB-COMMITTEE OF THE UNIT RESOURCE DEVELOPMENT COMMITTEE

TO: The Board Membership Sub-Committee of the Resource Development Committee

FROM: The Resource Development Committee

General Commission

The Board Membership Sub-Committee is commissioned by and responsible to the Resource Development Committee of Unit One of the Newport Organization to assume the primary relationship to matters pertaining to Board of Managers' recruitment, orientation, motivation, and evaluation in accordance with established policies and practices approved by the Corporate Board of the Newport Organization.

Appointments and Composition

1. The appointment of the Chairperson of the Board Membership Sub-Committee is to be made by the Chairperson of the Unit Resource Development Committee for the ensuing year. This appointment is to be made in consultation with the Chairperson of the Board of Managers.

2. Other members of this Committee are to be selected at a meeting of the Board Chairperson, Resource Development Committee Chairperson and the Board Membership Sub-Committee Chairperson.

Responsibilities

1. *Study* the composition of the Board, having in mind opti-

mum breadth of talents, skills, and capacity to assume all aspects of the Unit's success.

2. *On-going evaluation* of the present Board of Managers, always asking: "How can the talents of this person be better challenged for the benefit of Unit One?" Keep an on-going record of Board meeting attendance, Committee service, and evidence of commitment to the youth of Newport.

3. *Study* the Unit area proximity map to ensure that there is an executive representative of each major corporation serving on the Board.

4. *Nominate* for Board service such candidates as have a real contribution to make to the success of the Unit.

5. *Poll* the Board annually as to the areas of committee service each is best fitted for.

6. *Review* annually the procedures for Board recruitment.

*   *   *   *   *

COMMISSION FOR A PUBLIC RELATIONS SUB-COMMITTEE OF THE UNIT RESOURCE DEVELOPMENT COMMITTEE

TO: The Public Relations Sub-Committee of the Resource Development Committee

FROM: The Resource Development Committee

General Commission

The Public Relations Sub-Committee is commissioned by and is responsible to the Resource Development Committee of Unit One of the Newport Organization to assume the primary relationship to matters pertaining to public relations and publicity, enhancing the internal and external image of the Newport Organization in the area served by the Unit, and coordinating all matters pertaining to public relations and publicity with the Department of Resource Development in the Administrative Office of the Newport Organization.

Appointments and Composition

1. Appointments to the Public Relations Sub-Committee are made on an annual basis by the Chairperson of the Board of Managers and the Chairperson of the Resource Development Committee for the ensuing year.

2. The Chairperson of this subcommittee is to be a member of the Board of Managers.

3. Other members may be appointed from the community in accordance with particular capacity in specialized fields, with particular emphasis on persons with experience in the field of public relations or related areas of communication.

4. These members will be appointed by the Board Chairperson and the Resource Development Committee Chairperson upon recommendation of the Public Relations Subcommittee chairperson.

Responsibilities

1. *Develop* a complete program of public relations, promotion, and publicity for the Unit, projected for a one-year basis beginning each April.

2. *Establish and maintain* a good working relationship with the area media.

3. *Develop* a routine of coverage and information built around news events occurring at the Unit.

4. *Maintain* a liaison with the Department of Resource Development for the Newport Organization in developing and instituting long-range public relations programs.

NOMINATING COMMITTEE
MANUAL OF OPERATION
Appendix III

Manuals of operation contain recommended procedures for a committee to follow if it is to function effectively. One such manual is the *Nominating Committee Manual of Operation.*

This is a comparatively short manual because the nominating committee, as an ad hoc committee, has a short-term function. Other manuals of operation can be designed using this one as a format. As an example, Chapter 12, "The Board Membership Process," could be adapted as a manual of operation for the Board Membership Committee.

Interpretive Index

Commission for the Nominating Committee (Ad hoc)

This is the job description for your committee, spelling out your responsibilities and your place in the accountability pattern.

Criteria for Board Member Performance Evaluation

Board membership within the Newport Organization system involves a heavy and serious commitment. Evaluation criteria are necessary to determine whether or not a member should be asked to remain after his or her three-year term has expired.

Board Member Meeting and Activity Record

This recording sheet indicates the degree of participation of each board member and should be considered, along with other factors, in the renomination of Board personnel.

234

Board of Directors Individual Contribution Record

One important function of a member of the Board of Directors is helping to finance the work.

Master Schedule of Board and Committee Meetings

This is an index of total lay participation.

Annual Performance Evaluation of Board Members for Use of Nominating Committee

This is the recommendation of your committee regarding nomination and serves as the basis for Board action.

Nomination of Officers

Nominating of officers follows normal procedure in accordance with criteria.

*   *   *   *   *

COMMISSION FOR THE NOMINATING COMMITTEE.

TO: The Nominating Committee (ad hoc)

FROM: The Board of Directors

General Commission

The nominating Committee is commissioned by and responsible to the Board of Directors of the Newport Organization to prepare a single slate of all officers and members of the Board of Directors whose terms expire and to file such slate with the Executive Director no later than thirty (30) days prior to the November business meeting.

Appointments and Composition

1. The Nominating Committee is elected in September of each year.

2. The Committee is composed of members of the Board of Directors whose terms of office do not expire in that given year.

3. The Committee, at its first meeting, will elect a Chairperson.

Responsibilities

To evaluate carefully the performance of each Board member,

recommend candidates for office, and prepare a slate of members for retention on the Board or to be dropped from the Board.

*   *   *   *   *

CRITERIA FOR BOARD MEMBER PERFORMANCE EVALUATION

NEWPORT ORGANIZATION
NOMINATING COMMITTEE

The success of the Newport Organization is based on the participation of its laymen. It is therefore crucial that the performance of each layman be evaluated by the Nominating Committee. Listed below are some suggested criteria for evaluating a Board member's performance:

1. Participation in fund raising

2. Material contributions

3. Board meetings attended

4. Committee meetings attended

5. Participation on ad hoc committees

6. Offices held

7. Recruitment of new Board members

8. Innovative ideas introduced

It is not possible to set uniform standards which fit all situations. Nominating committees, therefore, should weigh each criterion according to its conditions.

BOARD EVALUATION FORMS

1. Master Schedule of Board and Committee Meetings— Form 1.

2. Board Member Meeting and Activity Record—Form 2.

3. Board of Directors Individual Contribution Record—Form 3.

4. Annual Performance Evaluation of Board Members for Use of Nominating Committee—Form 4.

5. Nomination of Officers—Form 5.

NEWPORT ORGANIZATION

BOARD OF DIRECTORS

MASTER SCHEDULE OF BOARD AND COMMITTEE MEETINGS

YEAR 19___

MEETINGS	JAN.	FEB.	MAR.	APR.	MAY	JUNE	JULY	AUG.	SEPT.	OCT.	NOV.	DEC.	MEETING TOTAL
BOARD													
COMMITTEES													
1. EXECUTIVE													
2. PROGRAM SERVICES													
3.													
4.													
5.													
6.													
7. RESOURCE DEVELOPMENT													
8. CAMPAIGN													
9. MEMBERSHIP													
10. PUBLIC RELATIONS													
11. FINANCE													
12. PROPERTY													
13. PERSONNEL													
14.													
15.													
MONTHLY TOTAL													

Form 1

NEWPORT ORGANIZATION

BOARD MEMBER MEETING AND ACTIVITY RECORD

NAME _____

UNIT _____

DATE ELECTED TO BOARD _____

MEETINGS	JAN.	FEB.	MAR.	APR.	MAY	JUNE	JULY	AUG.	SEPT.	OCT.	NOV.	DEC.	MEETINGS HELD	TOTAL ATTENDED
BOARD														
COMMITTEES														
1.														
2.														
3.														
4.														
CORPORATE MEETINGS ATTENDED														
SPECIAL EVENT PARTICIPATION														

OFFICES HELD   NEW BOARD MEMBERS RECRUITED   PROGRAMS OR SERVICES INITIATED   OTHER ACTIVITIES

_____   _____   _____   _____

_____   _____   _____   _____

_____   _____   _____   _____

_____   _____   _____   _____

Meeting Record: If board member attends, place date of meeting in under month.
Total number of meetings held is obtained from the Board and Committee
Meeting form.

Form 2

238

NEWPORT ORGANIZATION

BOARD OF DIRECTORS INDIVIDUAL CONTRIBUTION RECORD

NAME _____ UNIT _____ MEMBER SINCE _____

YEAR	CAMPAIGN			UNITS	WOMEN'S BOARD	SPECIAL EVENTS COMMITTEE	MATERIAL	NON-OPERATING	WILLS & BEQUESTS	TOTAL
	PERSONAL	COMPANY	RAISED							

Form 3

NEWPORT ORGANIZATION

ANNUAL PERFORMANCE EVALUATION OF BOARD MEMBERS FOR USE OF NOMINATING COMMITTEE

SUBMITTED TO BOARD OF DIRECTORS BY _____, CHAIRMAN   DATE _____

NAME	MEMBER SINCE	ACTION TAKEN		
		UNQUALIFIED RENOMINATION	PROGRAMMED RENOMINATION	PROGRAMMED SEPARATION

Form 4

240

NEWPORT ORGANIZATION

REPORT ON NOMINATION OF OFFICERS

Chairman of Board: _____

President: _____

Vice Presidents: _____

_____

_____

_____

_____

_____

Secretary: _____

Treasurer: _____

Other:

_____

_____

_____

_____

_____

_____

(To be submitted to Executive Director)

Form 5

Exhibit Availability
Appendix IV

Most exhibits are available in chart form.

1. Those *not* available:

   3-9
   12
   32-28
   70
   81-83

   91
   97-104

2. Available in oversize sheets:

9, 10, 11, 16	—11 " × 17 " sheet
17-23	—23 " × 34½" sheet
27, 28	—11 " × 17 " sheet
39, 40, 41, 42	—11 " × 17 " sheet
50, 51, 53, 54, 55, 56, 61-66	—17¼" × 21½" sheet

3. The rest are on 8½" × 11" sheets

   Write or call for costs to:

   Voluntary Management Press
   Box 9170
   Downers Grove, Illinois 60515
   (312) 454-0684

Bibliography
Appendix V

Books and Pamphlets

Church, David M. *How to Succeed with Volunteers.* New York: National Public Relations Council of Health & Welfare Services, Inc., 1962.

Dapper, Gloria, and Carter, Barbara. *A Guide for School Board Members.* Chicago: Follett Publishing Company, 1966.

Gardner, John W. *Self-Renewal: The Individual and the Innovative Society.* New York: Harper & Row, 1964.

Greenleaf, Robert K. *The Institution as Servant.* Cambridge, Massachusetts: Center for Applied Studies, 1972.

———. *The Servant as Leader.* Cambridge, Massachusetts: Center for Applied Studies, 1970.

———. *Trustees as Servants.* Cambridge, Massachusetts: Center for Applied Studies, 1975.

Hanson, Pauline L., and Marmaduke, Carolyn T. *THE BOARD MEMBER—Decision Maker for the Nonprofit Corporation.* Sacramento, California: Han-Mar Publications, 1972.

Hasenfeld, Yeheskel, and English, Richard A. *Human Service Organizations.* Ann Arbor: University of Michigan Press, 1974.

Herron, Orley R. *The Role of the Trustee.* Scranton, Pennsylvania: International Textbook Company, 1969.

Houle, Cyril O. *The Effective Board.* New York: Association Press, 1960.

Koontz, Harold. *The Board of Directors and Effective Management.* New York: McGraw-Hill, 1967.

Lindeman, Edward. *The Community: An Introduction to the Study of Community Leadership and Organization.* New York: Association Press, 1961.

Naylor, Harriet H. *Volunteers Today.* Dryden Associates, 1973.

O'Connell, Brian. *Effective Leadership in Voluntary Organizations: How to Make the Greatest Use of Citizen Service and Influence.* New York: Association Press, 1976.

Ross, Joel E., and Kami, Michael S. *Corporate Management in Crisis: Why The Mighty Fall.* Englewood Cliffs, N. J.: Prentice-Hall, Inc., 1973.

Schindler-Rainman, Eva, and Lippitt, Ronald. *The Volunteer Community: Creative Use of Human Resources.* Fairfax, Virginia: NTL/Learning Resources Corp. 1976.

Seymour. *Designs for Fund-raising: Principles, Patterns, Techniques.* New York: McGraw-Hill, 1966.

Sorenson, Ray. *How To Be a Board or Committee Member.* New York: Association Press, 1962.

Sprafkin, Benjamin. *How To Become a More Effective Board Member.* Social Life Series, Richmond School of Social Work, Virginia Commonwealth University (March–April, 1968).

Trecker, Harleigh B. *Citizen Boards at Work.* New York: Association Press, 1970.

———, and Trecker, Audrey R. *Working with Groups, Committees and Communities.* New York: Association Press/Follet Publishing Company, 1980.